Connecting Primary Ma...

Connecting Primary Maths & Science

A Practical Approach

Alan Cross and Alison Borthwick

Mc Graw Hill Education Open University Press

Open University Press
McGraw-Hill Education
8th Floor
338 Euston Road
London
NW1 3BH

email: enquiries@openup.co.uk
world wide web: www.openup.co.uk

and Two Penn Plaza, New York, NY 10121-2289, USA

First published 2016

A catalogue record of this book is available from the British Library

ISBN-13: 1 978-0-33-526188-8
ISBN-10: 0-33-526188-4
eISBN: 978-0-33-526189-2

Library of Congress Cataloging-in-Publication Data
CIP data applied for

Typeset by Aptara, Inc.

Praise for this Book

"This book makes a useful contribution to primary STEM education. It makes a case for closer integration of maths and science, recognising that science provides contexts for mathematics and that mathematics is a necessary tool for any scientific enquiry.

It connects the two disciplines at surface and deep levels, illustrating how maths can be applied to science and how science provides a chance for mathematics to be applied, and drawing out the parallels between working mathematically and scientifically.

The book respects the distinctiveness of each discipline: chapters provide accessible surveys of content and examples of classroom activities in both areas."

Miles Berry, University of Roehampton, UK

Contents

Acknowledgements

The authors would like to thank:

David, Hannah and Sue for their support

Joanne Graveling for the pencil sketches of the mathematicians and scientists

Russell Rukin for the artwork of the human hand skeleton

And the following schools:

Heathfield Primary School, Bolton
Bradshaw Hall Primary School, Stockport
Mauldeth Road Primary School, Manchester
Bawdeswell Primary School, Norfolk
Caister Junior School, Norfolk
Chapel Break Infant School, Norfolk
Frettenham Primary School, Norfolk
Hillside Avenue Primary and Nursery School, Norfolk
Martham Primary and Nursery School, Norfolk
St. Augustine's Catholic Primary School, Norfolk

1

Introduction: Connecting Primary Mathematics and Science Education

> The development of scientifically and mathematically informed citizens is of such importance that it needs to begin in earnest during primary education in order to help ensure children have the best possible start in life and continued throughout secondary education. (The Royal Society, 2014)

This book is for teachers with an interest in primary mathematics and science education. It focuses on how these two subjects can and should be connected and shows what it is to work scientifically and mathematically. Many people regard mathematics 'to be a body of established knowledge and procedures – facts and rules' (Ahmed, 1987). While there are elements of this within learning mathematics, using science reveals how mathematics contributes to real life situations, enhancing and enriching the learning of both subjects. In what we might call our scientific world, there are no areas where mathematics is not present! To some, making links between these subjects feels intuitive. However, learners often view these two subjects as being separate and discrete, perhaps as a result of the way that school systems organise the curricula. It is our aim within this book to show that by connecting these subjects you and each learner can be both scientist and mathematician. This book in no way advocates the dilution of either subject. Science and mathematics remain pillars of human thought and creativity. Each offers a powerful set of knowledge, understanding and skills but together form a formidable corpus of human achievement with advances to come that we cannot imagine. Will the learners in our classes make discoveries? Contribute to the advancement of humanity? Will they be motivated to use mathematics and science in their lives? These subjects should be part of every child's education and ought to be integrated to enhance their meaning to all learners.

Why make connections?

Science and mathematics are important STEM subjects (find out more at http://www.stemnet.org.uk) and will be pivotally important in the lives of your learners and the society in which they live. Both subjects are essential in helping all of us to understand the world. This book shows primary teachers how straightforward, enjoyable and rewarding linking mathematics and science can be.

When planning lessons, you will have a choice of contexts for investigations and problem solving. Make sure that you include ones that enable strong links between science and mathematics. A report published by The Royal Society (2014) outlined its vision for the next twenty years to unite science and mathematics education. With the Royal Society's fundamental purpose to recognise, promote and support excellence in mathematics and science, this report is timely with its vision to promote the integration of both subjects through education. The report is very clear, however, that nurturing scientific and mathematical thinking needs to begin at primary school. Forging these links early on is likely to have a long-lasting impact on learner attitudes towards these two subjects. The Royal Society (2014) usefully summarises what it is to be a scientifically informed individual and a mathematically informed individual. The capacities listed in Table 1.1 are remarkable in the way the subjects complement one another.

Like The Royal Society, Haylock insists that links between subjects like mathematics and science are essential: 'The skills of handling data and pictorial representation are best taught through purposeful enquiries related to topics focusing on other areas of the curriculum, such as … science' (Haylock, 2010). The contribution of mathematics to science education has always been important but never more so than now. Feasey and Gallear (2000) recognised the need for this but also the power of numerate individuals to engage in both subjects. The National Curriculum (DfE, 2013) also recognises the importance of connecting the two subjects through applying 'mathematical knowledge' (DfE, 2013) in science while recognising that mathematics is 'critical to science' (DfE, 2013). Connecting mathematics and science can create opportunities within a curriculum to enhance learners' mathematics and science knowledge. For example, the latest version of the National Curriculum (DfE, 2013) does not include statistics within Year 1 mathematics even though young learners are required to work scientifically at this age, which requires them to gather and record data. This connection between mathematics and science allows Year 1 learners to work with simple data in meaningful and playful contexts (e.g. to record the daily weather). This gives them the chance to collect and record data in a memorable and enjoyable way. Such mathematical work in Year 1 would represent an improvement on the National Curriculum (DfE, 2013).

Researchers and writers talk about the importance of making connections between mathematics and science, often surmising that it is effective teachers who recognise and exploit this connectionist approach to learning (Askew et al., 1997). According to Haylock and Cockburn (2008), learning without making

Table 1.1 What it means to be scientifically and mathematically informed

A scientifically informed individual:	*A mathematically informed individual:*
1. understands scientific theories and concepts and that these are subject to challenge and changes as new evidence arises; 2. can think and act scientifically (e.g. using hypotheses to test and solve problems while also using scientific knowledge) and uses essential reading, writing, mathematical and communication skills to analyse scientific information accurately; 3. makes informed interpretations and judgements (e.g. risk assessment) about scientific information and the world at large as well as engaging in debate on scientific issues; 4. is able to apply scientific knowledge and understanding in everyday life; and 5. maintains curiosity about the natural and made worlds.	1. understands mathematical concepts and recognises when they are present; 2. can think and act mathematically (e.g. applying knowledge and transforming methods to solve problems), and uses mathematical skills and forms of communication to analyse situations within mathematics and elsewhere; 3. can make informed interpretations of information presented in a mathematical form and use it to engage constructively in debate on scientific and other issues; 4. is able to apply mathematical knowledge and understanding in everyday life; and 5. maintains curiosity in mathematical concepts, and in other phenomena understood from a mathematical perspective.

Source: The Royal Society (2014)

connections is tantamount to 'rote learning'. Others (Ofsted, 2008; Williams, 2008) observe that the use and application of mathematics is not always embedded in classroom practice. Science provides the perfect medium through which to offer these opportunities. Indeed, Treffers and Beishuizen (in Thompson, 1999) encourage children to be purposefully engaged in problem-solving tasks. Investigation enables science and mathematics learning, as they both require real-life enquiry, reasoning and problem solving. In an article about teaching mathematics creatively, Naik includes a case study of a teacher who was 'very keen that mathematics work should be linked closely with that of science, noting that there are many natural connections which should be capitalised on' (Naik, 2013), such as extrapolating from a set of data.

Mathematics and science share an interest in numeric and other relationships. It is worth emphasising that in science we aim for a number of things. Science enquiry is greatly enhanced through the measurement, control and systematic change of variables in an experiment or test. Thus an important step in primary science is the shift from simple observation of phenomena to increasingly

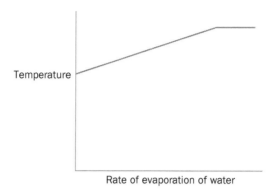

Rate of evaporation of water

Figure 1.1 Graph showing the rate of evaporation of water as the temperature of the water increases to boiling point

accurate quantitative measurement and increasingly sophisticated use of data in addressing questions to establish, for example, causal relationships. This is very well exemplified by the use of tables and graphs (Goldsworthy et al., 1999), especially line graphs which represent a relationship between two variables (e.g. as temperature increases towards boiling point, so does the rate of evaporation of water; see Figure 1.1).

Well-organised, purposeful curricular links between subjects allow children's learning to be extended and deepened (Barnes, 2011; Hendry, 2013; Rose, 2009). According to Ofsted (2010), this approach affords opportunities for independent enquiry that can be inclusive and relevant for all learners. As professional educators we should take care. John Hattie has reviewed research on integrated curricula and noted that any positive effect can vary from subject to subject, with mathematics benefiting more than science in one enquiry. Overall, however, he noted that integration had a greater positive effect in primary education (Hattie, 2009). This book recognises the value of subjects as one way (Alexander, 2010) – we would say, a very powerful way – of organising human knowledge. For learning to be meaningful, we consider that curricular links and connections can assist learners making sense of the world.

Working scientifically or working mathematically?

One of the strongest connections between mathematics and science is seen in how learners work scientifically and mathematically. Working as a mathematician or as a scientist requires a curious and enquiring mind, which observes the world and asks why, how, could, should and would? It is like wearing a special pair of glasses, through which is viewed a world of questions and enquiries. With this curiosity in place, questions can be posed, conjectures proved or disproved, hypotheses tested, rules and theorems established.

In the science curriculum (DfE, 2013), working scientifically precedes the blocks of knowledge within each key stage. Many learners come to science with ideas and interpretations concerning the phenomena that they are studying. They often form these ideas as a result of everyday experiences. The objectives of the working scientifically programmes of study (DfE, 2013) aim to harness, shape and develop the skills and understanding needed to test and interpret science ideas. For example, they remind us to ask questions, gather data and perform comparative and fair tests while learning about living things, materials or physical processes. Working scientifically includes the core characteristics of being a scientist, and reflects the three aims of the science curriculum (developing science knowledge and conceptual understanding; developing understanding of the nature, processes and methods of science; understanding the use and implications of science). However, the list of objectives within the working scientifically programmes of study (DfE, 2013) are so mathematical it would not be a surprise to find them in the mathematics curriculum. Consider these examples from the science programme of study:

- identifying and classifying;
- gathering and recording data to help in answering questions;
- using results to draw simple conclusions;
- reporting on findings from enquiries, including oral and written explanations, displays or presentations of results and conclusions;
- taking measurements. (DfE, 2013)

The mathematics programme of study (DfE, 2013), however, does not mirror the science programme of study in that there is no separate section for working mathematically. Instead, working mathematically is contained within the three aims of the mathematics curriculum (fluency, reasoning and problem solving). Historically, there has always been a working mathematically strand in previous versions of the mathematics curriculum (e.g. DfEE, 1999), although it has appeared under various pseudonyms such as using and applying mathematics, or problem solving. However, our purpose in including working mathematically (Chapter 2) remains the same, in that to be a successful learner in mathematics requires understanding and skills that allow us to solve problems, to enquire, to reason and justify, and to communicate and explain. Just as science education would be meaningless without working scientifically, mathematics education would lack meaning and purpose if we did not teach the understanding, skills and processes alongside the content. Jones (2003) writes that 'a mathematics curriculum without problem solving can be likened to a diet of PE in which children practise football and netball skills but never get to play a game'. Within the mathematics curriculum (DfE, 2013) we need to look to the three aims of fluency, reasoning and problem solving to provide this element. Chapter 2 offers further discussion on working mathematically, while Chapter 9 unpicks what it is to work scientifically.

Table 1.2 Science and mathematical skills

Science skills	Mathematics skills*
• observing • asking questions • hypothesising • investigating • communicating and reflecting • interpreting evidence, drawing conclusions	• procedural recall, accuracy and fluency of number • interpretation and use of concrete, pictorial and abstract representations • application of mathematical knowledge and experience • strategies for problem solving and hypothesis testing • mathematical reasoning • appreciation of the purpose and usefulness of mathematics, and willingness to use it

*Based on the skills identified by ACME (2011)

Mathematical and scientific skills

Mathematics and science are both subjects that require a specific set of skills and knowledge in order for learners to be successful. This section looks at how the skills of mathematics and science are more connected than perhaps we thought. However, we first summarise the skills associated within each subject (Table 1.2) before considering the connections between them.

How do these skills connect?

Is it possible that these so-called mathematics skills and science skills are in fact one set of skills? These skills are about perceiving what is going on in the world, establishing relationships, making things predictable and using this to either expand knowledge and understanding or in other ways improve life. Looking at the two sets of skills, it is hard to detect many differences between the skills of learning science and those of learning mathematics. Figure 1.2 shows the considerable overlap that exists. There are marked similarities between the two sets of skills. We suspect many people would not be able to decide whether 'investigating' or 'problem solving and hypothesis testing' are mathematical or science skills! We would also suggest that being aware of these skills and connecting the subjects in this way actually enhances learning, not only because learners have more opportunities to practise and use these skills but also because subject-specific skills in one subject enrich the other.

As well as understanding the similarities between the skills within each subject, the opportunities that subject-specific content and activities afford also adds to these curricular connections. Schoenfeld (1994) makes the distinction between learning mathematics and doing mathematics. While there is a need for pupils to learn mathematical content and knowledge, there is also the need for them to apply and practise these skills. Science investigation provides the perfect

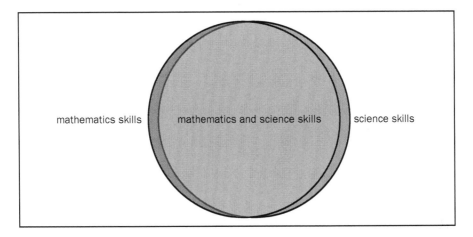

mathematics skills   mathematics and science skills   science skills

Figure 1.2 Most science and mathematics skills are shared

vehicle for many of these skills. Practising mathematical skills in a real-world context not only reinforces these skills but helps to extend and deepen knowledge. Learners make more of science and mathematics when they have posed questions about a topic and then sought answers themselves. This approach enables the use of mathematical and scientific language, makes links very clear and aids the development of skills. Spendlove and Cross (2013) note that 'learning through doing is both rich in content and process'. Science provides the ideal context to harness the skills learnt through mathematical problem solving, but in a real-life context. Mathematics provides science with a means of describing, quantifying and articulating ideas and relationships. Progress in science education in the primary years can be seen as moving from predominantly qualitative observation, exploration and description towards increasingly planned, careful and precise quantitative methods.

So, there are many areas in the mathematics and science curriculum that overlap and use the same skills and knowledge. It is these areas that we wish to exploit in this book. We acknowledge that there needs to be episodes of discrete mathematics and science subject teaching. For example, learners may need to practise pattern spotting in shape or explore using hand lenses before embarking on a nature hunt. We are not advocating that every mathematics or science lesson adopt full integration. However, we will show, through the activities in the following chapters, that there are many opportunities where connecting the subjects is natural, adds value to the learning and makes sense.

Connecting through STEM

A number of schools have adopted a STEM (Science, Technology, Engineering and Mathematics) approach (Figure 1.3). This varies but involves to some extent

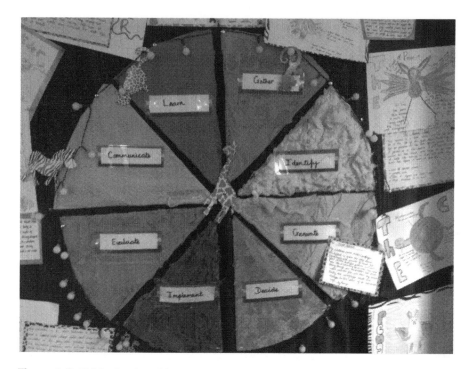

Figure 1.3 TASC wheel enables primary learners who are working across the STEM subjects

or another integrating these subjects across the entire curriculum or in a number of themes or topics that are developed. Primary schools use a primary STEM approach to ensure that science, design and technology, computing and mathematics combine in all sorts of ways. A STEM approach encourages learners to see and use links across the four subjects and many of the contexts we develop in this book would be ideal for this approach.

One primary school uses the TASC (Thinking Activity in a Social Context) wheel (Wallace et al., 2008) to scaffold learners' thought around different topics and problems that link science, mathematics, and design and technology. In a water topic, learners designed a rain harvester to reduce the mains water required in the school garden (Figure 1.4). Learners made plans and designed model rainfall harvesters. This involved science, mathematics, design and technology, and computing. Find out more about TASC at http://tascwheel.com/?page_id=289. A host of primary STEM projects are available at http://www.nationalstemcentre.org.uk/elibrary/ and primary STEM ambassadors are available to visit schools for free. Find out more at http://www.stem.org.uk.

Figure 1.4 Learners construct a rainfall harvester

Organisation and structure of the book

The seven mathematics and eight science chapters that follow were designed to reflect the latest version of the English National Curriculum (DfE, 2013), and as such offer support in all areas for mathematics and science. In addition, we felt it important to include a mathematics chapter that focused on pattern. While this is not an explicit area within the latest mathematics curriculum (DfE, 2013), it is a theme that is important to both mathematics and science. Each chapter utilises the following elements.

Overview

As science and mathematics must always remain subjects in their own right, we have structured the book so that those readers looking for mathematics-led integration or for science-led integration can turn to chapters that deal with all the major topic areas taught in the two subjects. The book can be read from cover to cover but is also organised so that teachers can seek advice and ideas linked to aspects they are planning to teach. Each chapter begins with a brief overview, which offers a definition of the science or mathematics area and where relevant references to the National Curriculum (DfE, 2013).

Mathematicians and scientists

One way the chapters emphasise the links between the subjects is to celebrate the work of influential mathematicians and scientists. Each chapter refers to a person who has affected the world we live in and to whom science and mathematics were very important. These people laid some of the foundations for scientific and mathematical ideas or developed significant applications of mathematics and science. They gained fame along the way and we have tried to give a flavour of their contribution so that teachers can make use of them as inspirational figures to learners.

Within each chapter you will find reference to people such as Euclid, Newton, Pythagoras, Edison and Fibonacci. However, you may wonder why men dominate these examples, especially in mathematics. This is not because men are better at mathematics or science! It is because until very recently society held the view that it was not very respectable for women to pursue these subjects. However, there were a few women who dared to go against this view and their achievements have contributed greatly to their discipline. For example, Caroline Herschel was a mathematician and scientist, and the sister of the famous astronomer, William Herschel, credited with discovering the planet Uranus. Caroline worked alongside her brother and is reported to have completed most of the complicated mathematical calculations. Mary Somerville was another accomplished mathematician who translated and also added some original thoughts to some work by a French mathematician called Laplace. Ada Lovelace was the daughter of the famous poet Lord Byron. Taught by Mary Somerville, Lovelace worked alongside and supported Charles Babbage on the theoretical principles of the Analytical Engine, which Lovelace realised could be automated, and she is now regarded as one of the earliest pioneers of computer programming. The mathematicians and scientists we have chosen have contributed to some of the most amazing discoveries of all time. We have included examples of men and women so as to counteract gendering of mathematics and science.

Connecting mathematics and science

These sections draw links between the two subjects within the specific topic area. While we acknowledge that not all mathematics and science connect, we hope that you will be delighted by the extent to which they do.

Real-life examples

We particularly wanted to offer examples where science and mathematics have worked together in a real-life context. This we feel aids recognition that the mathematics and science we learn in school is used in the real world! So in the following chapters you will find examples within roller coasters, space shuttles and even the food industry.

Key teaching points

This section pinpoints some of the essential knowledge needed to teach the particular area of focus. It is not meant to be a comprehensive guide to subject knowledge but serves as a reminder. For a stronger focus on subject knowledge, we would recommend Cross and Bowden's (2014) *Essential Primary Science* or Haylock's (2010) *Mathematics Explained for Primary Teachers*.

Teaching activities

Each chapter then offers Key Stage 1 and 2 teaching activities. We have used two contexts within each key stage to show how these subjects could link within the subject-specific area. In mathematics, the first context includes an activity where the two subjects work in unison to achieve the learning, while the second context offers a mathematics-led activity, followed by a science-led activity. This decision is purposeful and acknowledges that while a context may offer links between the two subjects, sometimes it is best for one subject to lead. This approach can be adapted to suit your lessons. It is the context that connects the subjects and so the activities that follow offer you an opportunity to exploit these links. The contexts within the science chapters focus solely on integrating science and mathematics simultaneously. This is because the subjects complement one another so naturally. In each case, we have provided the National Curriculum references from the programme of study (DFE, 2013).

Conclusion and summary

These two short sections offer a quick guide to the overall content within the chapter and so serve as a useful reminder or a quick check for readers.

Terminology

A number of terms are used in mathematics and science about which you as a teacher should be clear. In science, the following terms sometimes cause confusion. These are test, experiment and investigation. The first of these, *test*, can be the smallest in terms of action, and is often an instance where phenomena are observed in controlled conditions, for example a parachute is dropped from 1.5 m or a seedling is grown in sand for ten days. An *experiment* may be straightforward but can involve a number of tests so that a set of results are collected. An experiment may have a science question, a prediction, results and conclusion. An *investigation* in science may include one or more tests and even one or more experiments, such as an investigation into the characteristics of fabrics for clothing a toddler.

The following terms overlap strongly between science and mathematics, but it is important that they are used correctly.

Questions: Questions are important in both subjects and can be used to initiate thought about a phenomenon or relationship to be investigated.

Predictions: Predictions are routinely used in science to say, based on present understanding, what might happen. In mathematics, this is akin to estimation where we might consider a question and then roughly consider a likely outcome, for example $1.5 \times 5.5 =$ approximately 8.

Conjecture: A conjecture is a hypothesis. It is a statement that may be proved right or wrong, such as: all quadrilaterals have equal sides; some hours are longer than others; only reptiles and birds lay eggs; Venus is always the first new bright natural shining object in the evening sky.

Hypothesis: A hypothesis is a rule that we might hope to establish as a generalisation, law or theorem, for example all yellow boats float. It has to be tested and only after sufficient evidence has been gathered can it be accepted and promoted to a law.

Reasoning: Reasoning is a form of thinking that employs logic, for example all these plants are green, so all plants are green.

Generalisation: A generalisation is a statement which is true or correct and which applies across all known instances, for example: an odd number plus an odd number always equals an even number; a solute will dissolve into a solvent until the solution is saturated; warmer air holds more moisture; the further we are from a light source, the less bright the light; as speed increases, travel time is reduced.

Rule: This is another word for a generalisation or a law.

Law: A law in science is the statement of a generalisation based on the best evidence to date. A law in science is only as good as the evidence that confirms it. Once contradictory evidence is found, the law has to be rewritten or replaced.

Theorem: A theorem is a proven rule or relationship in mathematics. To become a theorem, a statement must be proved – that is, in all examples the statement is proven. For example, in right-angled triangles the square of the hypotenuse is equal to the sum of the squares of the other two sides.

Conclusion

Links between mathematics and science often appear very natural but in an educational context it is worthwhile taking a systematic approach so that all the benefits available are taken. Cross-referencing the curriculum is one way to do this, as is an organised approach to developing science and mathematical skills. Each subject is powerful in its own right, but the learning of both subjects can be enhanced through integrated approaches.

Summary of learning

In this chapter, you should have learned:

- about the interrelatedness of mathematics and science;
- that connections made between mathematics and science enrich both subjects;
- about the skills of mathematics and science;
- about the structure of this book.

2

Working Mathematically

This chapter will ensure that you:

- have a secure understanding of what it means to work mathematically;

- understand the connections between working scientifically and working mathematically.

Overview

While the science curriculum (DfE, 2013) explicitly refers to skills learners need to explore and understand in science through the programmes of study on working scientifically, the mathematics curriculum is less explicit about the mathematical skills to be learned. However, they can be found in the aims of the mathematics curriculum (DfE, 2013) and reside firmly within fluency, reasoning and problem solving. We have chosen to refer to these aims as 'working mathematically' in this book to emphasise this parity between science and mathematics in the skills they use (as well as subject-specific content). Looking at the content linked to the mathematics aims and to working scientifically, it is hard not to see the connections between the two disciplines. Gathering and recording data to help answer questions would seem to be a mathematical skill (which of course it is), yet it appears in the Key Stage 1 section on working scientifically (DfE, 2013). Similarly, following a line of enquiry or developing an argument could just as easily be a science skill, yet it is part of the reasoning aim in the mathematics curriculum.

Fluency, reasoning and problem solving represent the application of mathematics (or working mathematically) in the latest version of the English National Curriculum (NC) (DfE, 2013). Over the years, phrases such as using and applying, investigations and solving problems have also been used, but essentially all represent the same concept: being a successful learner is about using and applying mathematical content in a meaningful and purposeful way.

Teachers will interpret the aims in their own way, but fluency is essentially about seeing links and forming relationships between numbers or values. We often talk about fluency in relation to number because this is the largest part of the mathematics curriculum, but there are other areas where fluency is important too (e.g. being fluent in choosing which measuring equipment to use or whether to use a graph or chart to present data). Russell (2000) suggests that fluency has three elements to it: efficiency, accuracy and flexibility. Thus, fluency is more than memorising a single procedure or stumbling towards an answer.

Reasoning is often referred to 'the "glue" which helps mathematics make sense' (Pennant et al., 2014). It could also be thought of as mathematical thinking where learners have to think and reason through mathematical problems to try and make sense of them or convince others their approach is logical and their answer correct. There are many levels to reasoning. For example, learners may start to reason by simply describing what they did, before moving on to offer reasons, finding a chain of logical reasoning or even a proof! Nunes et al. (2009) identified the ability to reason mathematically as the most important factor in a pupil's success in mathematics. One of their key findings showed that mathematical reasoning is even more important than learners' knowledge of arithmetic for later achievement in mathematics.

Problem solving is vast! It is also the point and purpose of doing mathematics. There are many different types of problems (e.g. word problems, logical problems, finding all the possibilities), so it is often better to think of the skills associated with problem solving. This is because learners can sometimes engage with a problem without actually solving it! Again this list is extensive, so we will focus on the ones that link strongly between science and mathematics:

- trial and improvement;
- looking for patterns;
- working systematically;
- working backwards;
- conjecturing and convincing;
- logical reasoning.

There are many definitions of problem solving. However, we have chosen to follow Polya, who has formulated one of the most publicised and published principles for problem solving. For Polya (1945), problem solving is:

- seeking solutions not just memorising procedures;
- exploring patterns not just memorising formulas;
- formulating conjectures, not just doing exercises.

Learners need to have a mathematical toolkit of approaches to solving a problem and know how and when to use them.

Teaching tip

For further discussion on fluency, reasoning and problem solving, see the nrich website at www.nrich.org.uk

Although mathematics does not have an equivalent section with explicit objectives like working scientifically in the science curriculum (DfE, 2013), fluency, reasoning and problem solving help to show what working mathematically entails. In fact, it is hard for learners not to work mathematically in their everyday lives. The boy shown in Figure 2.1 is demonstrating mathematical fluency by working out the number sequence, by reasoning which number to hop to next, that will help him to solve the problem in the game of hopscotch.

Working scientifically and working mathematically are more closely linked than perhaps we think. We might assume that we are working scientifically when we are collecting data and hypothesising about the amount of rainfall in one week, but we are also using our fluency skills to make sense of the numbers, our reasoning skills to offer explanations as to why one area had more rain than another, and our problem-solving skills to plan, report and present the findings from our experiment; in other words, we are working mathematically too. Having knowledge of science and mathematical skills and using it across both

Figure 2.1 Working mathematically to play hopscotch

subjects only strengthens learners' understanding of each. Working mathematically has enabled science to change our lives. How can mathematics and science not be connected in a national curriculum?

An example of a mathematician

Charles Lutwidge Dodgson, better known as Lewis Carroll, was born in Daresbury, Cheshire, England (Figure 2.2). Dodgson taught mathematics at Oxford but is often better remembered for his books, *Alice's Adventures in Wonderland* (2001) and *Alice Through the Looking Glass* (2008). Hidden within the stories are many mathematical and scientific concepts and ideas, including when Alice shrinks and her proportions are all wrong, and when she tries to remember her multiplication tables in the hallway but they had slipped out of the base ten number system we use today.

One school used the story of Alice to inspire a whole context around 'Alice in Numberland'. Figure 2.3 shows how learners were investigating odd and even numbers, a key area of fluency within working mathematically.

You could also use *Alice's Adventures in Wonderland* (2001) to talk about the passage of time. One type of scientific enquiry includes observing over time and

Figure 2.2 Pencil sketch of Charles Dodgson (1832–1898)

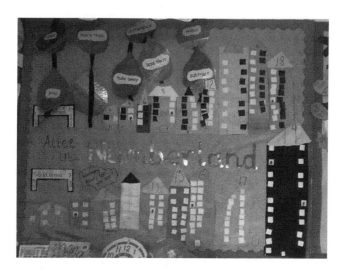

Figure 2.3 Alice in Numberland

seeking answers to questions. How long was Alice underground for? How many hours, minutes, seconds? What could we do in an hour or a minute? Or you could use it as a link to make some clocks, just like the learners did in Figure 2.4. Notice how the clocks have linked to understanding fractions too. Making connections is an important skill that helps learners to be fluent and reason about the connections that appear continually in mathematics and science.

As well as many mathematical links, there are also some interesting, underlying concepts regarding scientific theories too. For example, the story assumes

Figure 2.4 Clocks inspired by the White Rabbit

Table 2.1 Interesting facts about square numbers

First square	Second square	Sum of squares	Double of sum	Expressed as sum of two squares
4	9	13	26	1 + 25
25	64	89	178	9 + 169
4	16	20	40	4 + 36

that Alice was asleep and is just remembering her dreams as she awakes. We could ask learners to consider whether our dreams are fact or fiction. What constitutes a fact? How is it that we often remember dreams so vividly, just as if they were real?

Another reason to include Dodgson in this chapter was his collection of logic games and puzzles. One of his discoveries related to square numbers. He found that doubling the sum of two square numbers could always be expressed as the sum of two square numbers (Table 2.1). These sorts of problems encourage the learners to use their fluency and reasoning skills as well as problem skills of recording systematically and thinking logically.

Connecting mathematics and science: working mathematically

The skills learners use to work mathematically are very similar to the ones used in working scientifically. In this way, mathematics and science are inseparable. Learners often cannot distinguish whether a pond dipping activity is science or mathematics. However, the questions they ask, the reasons they come up with, the way they use their observations to suggest answers or solve problems are just as much mathematical as they are scientific. Working across the curriculum capitalises on these opportunities and helps to develop knowledge, skills and understanding in a stronger way because learners are using them in a stimulating, wide-ranging and connected way. Teachers could actively pursue mathematics using such contexts (e.g. devising questions related to number or geometry in the pond world) and in doing so connect easily with science.

A real-life example with mathematics and science

It would seem that both children and adults either love or hate roller coasters! There are many who flock to theme parks every year to try the tallest, fastest or scariest ride. But have you ever thought about the mathematics and science behind how roller coasters work?

The mathematical challenges involved in building a roller coaster depend on solving many problems along the way. For example, before companies can invest in building a ride, they need to work out whether it is worth it financially. They have to consider how many people they can take on one ride, how many times the ride can operate each hour, and the cost per person for each ride, which is then used to calculate how much revenue the ride could generate each hour, day and year.

For the scientists, one of the requirements is how to make the roller coaster move. Unlike a train, a roller coaster has no engine, and for most of the ride it is moved by gravity and momentum. However, it first needs to gain momentum by getting to the top of the hill. Traditionally, a chain is wound around a gear at the top of the hill to move the carriages up like a conveyor belt. Once at the top momentum and gravity take over, until the carriages reach the bottom and the chain mechanism takes over again. Without mathematics and science working together, we might not have the thrills of the roller coaster!

Key teaching points for working mathematically

The following are some of the key qualities that learners require to work mathematically:

- resilience;
- perseverance;
- determination;
- making observations;
- the ability to make mistakes and learn from them;
- identifying similarities and differences;
- being able to record solutions in different ways.

This list is not comprehensive but it provides an idea of the types of skills learners need within this area. These are all challenging skills to acquire. Learners often wrongly assume that school mathematics is about arriving at the answer quickly. Problems that have more than one answer, or that take a little longer to solve, often result in learners becoming frustrated or lacking in confidence.

One of the ways to support learners is to scaffold their development through questions:

- What happens when we ...?
- How many different ways can you find ...?
- How do you know you have got them all?
- How many different ... can you find?
- Have we done one like this before?
- What is the same/different?
- Do you see a pattern?
- What do you think comes next?

- Why do you think that?
- What have you discovered?
- Is there another way we could do this?
- Are everybody's solutions the same?
- Are you able to draw a picture to help you?

As discussed earlier, working mathematically presents itself through the three aims of the mathematics curriculum (DfE, 2013): fluency, reasoning and problem solving. This means that very few objectives appear in the programmes of study for working mathematically (DfE, 2013). Therefore, the activities that follow draw on content-led mathematics objectives, but throughout links are made as to how each activity draws on skills for both working mathematically and working scientifically.

Teaching activities linking mathematics to science

Key Stage 1

Topic: The king has lost his crown!

Activity: Design a crown fit for a king or queen

A letter arrives at school asking learners for their help. It is from King Arnold who has lost his crown. He asks the learners to use their mathematical and science skills to make a new one, but there are several rules they need to follow.

Rule number 1: The crown must have a circumference of 62 centimetres.

Rule number 2: The crown must be made of at least three different materials.

Rule number 3: The crown must include different shaped jewels and these need to be organised in a symmetrical pattern.

Rule number 4: The crown must be waterproof.

Rule number 5: Each child will be given £5 to buy the jewels with.

Rule number 6: Five smaller jewels can be exchanged for one larger jewel.

Rule number 7: The crown must be suitable to wear all year round.

Each rule draws on aspects of working scientifically and mathematically. For example, ensuring the crown must be waterproof will require learners to gather data about different materials, while using different shaped jewels utilises understanding of pattern within problem-solving skills.

This activity can be split over a number of days. It would be useful to have at least one session each on how to measure circumference and how to test which materials are waterproof before the learners begin to make the crowns.

NC mathematics objectives

- Solve one-step problems that involve addition and subtraction (Year 1 number – addition and subtraction);

- Compare, describe and solve practical problems for lengths and heights (Year 1 measurement);

- Identify and describe the properties of 2-D shapes, including the number of sides and line symmetry in a vertical line (Year 2 geometry – properties of shapes);

- Order and arrange combinations of mathematical objects in patterns and sequences (Year 2 geometry – position and direction).

NC science objectives

- Gather and record data to help in answering questions (Key Stage 1 working scientifically);

- Perform simple tests (Key Stage 1 working scientifically);

- Describe the physical properties of a variety of everyday materials (Year 1 everyday materials);

- Identify and compare the suitability of a variety of everyday materials, including wood, metal, plastic, glass, brick, rock, paper and cardboard for particular uses (Year 2 uses of everyday materials).

Teaching tip

It is even better if the king himself can visit the learners and discuss the rules with them!

Topic: Invertebrates

Mathematics-led activity: Centipede's shoes

This activity is based on the story *Centipede's 100 Shoes* (Ross, 2003). Begin the activity by discussing different types of invertebrates that learners know about (e.g. spiders, earthworms, centipedes). Ask learners how many legs they think the animals have. Record this information, but do not reveal the answers yet, as this is the science activity coming up!

In the story, the centipede hurts his toe and so decides to buy some shoes. He buys one hundred shoes as he thinks he has this many feet. As a class, decide how many legs your centipede will have. Let's choose fifty-eight. Set learners a number of challenges based on this centipede. For example:

1. If the centipede has fifty-eight feet, how many pairs of shoes do we need?

2. How many shoes and socks is that altogether?

3. If we bought one hundred pairs of shoes, how many would we have left over?

These questions allow learners to use their reasoning skills to convince each other about the number of shoes needed but also use their fluency skills to see relationships between numbers. Ask learners to come up with their own challenges for each other too. Remember to provide mathematical resources for learners to solve their problems with (e.g. counters, Numicon©, bead strings; see www.nrich.maths. org/10461 for more information on practical apparatus in mathematics lessons). For each question, ask learners to think how they will record their information, provide a reason for their approach and solution, and ultimately solve the problem, all of which support them in working mathematically.

NC mathematics objectives

- Count to and across 100 (Year 1 number – number and place value);

- Count in steps of 2, 3, and 5 from 0, and in tens from any number, forward and backward (Year 2 number – number and place value);

- Solve problems involving addition and subtraction (Year 1 and 2 number – addition and subtraction);

- Solve problems involving multiplication and division (Year 1 and 2 number – multiplication and division).

Science-led activity: Do all invertebrates have the same number of legs?

Return to the information learners provided on how many legs they think each of the invertebrates has. To begin, research how many legs each creature really does have. You could do this using live invertebrates (ensuring the learners treat them carefully), picture books or the internet. Different groups could make models of each invertebrate so the class has a visual aid to help them remember. Do all invertebrates have the same number of legs? Ensure that the learners know that a centipede only has forty-two legs, and not one hundred, as the story suggests! Using these methods, processes and skills supports learners to work scientifically too.

Once learners are armed with their information, take them outside to become explorers! Ask learners to look for invertebrates. They may start by observing signs of plants being eaten, or habitats invertebrates live in. If they find an invertebrate, take a photo of it. Back in the classroom, discuss where learners found them. What does this tell us about the habitats they choose?

NC science objectives

- Use their observations and ideas to suggest answers to questions (Key Stage 1 working scientifically);

- Gather and record data to help in answering questions (Key Stage 1 working scientifically);

- Identify and name a variety of common animals (Year 1 animals, including humans);

- Find out and describe the basic needs of animals, including humans, for survival (water, food and air) (Year 2 animals, including humans).

Key Stage 2

Topic: Noah's Ark

Activity: Which animals are aboard the ark?

This activity is based on the story of Noah and his ark. Challenge learners to discover how many animals are aboard the ark, what types of animals they are and, using this information, where they should be placed on the ark. In groups, give learners the total number of legs aboard the ark and let them investigate from here!

For example, you may tell one group that one hundred and fifty-five legs were seen boarding the ark, while another group has to work out the animals based on seventy-eight legs. Learners can choose which animals are on board, but encourage them to be systematic in their recording, so that they are able to convince the class at the end that their results are correct. Learners also need to think about the classification of the animals. It might help them when considering where to place the animals on the ark if they first classify the animals into vertebrates and invertebrates, for example. To solve this problem efficiently, learners need to use both their scientific and mathematical skills.

Once learners have finished, ask them to explain (reason) how they approached the task. Did they start, for example, by selecting the animals and then working out the numbers of legs, or solve the mathematics first by using multiples of numbers to represent numbers of legs (e.g. multiples of two, four, six and eight). If their total of legs was an odd number, what is their explanation for this (problem solving)?

Learners could also use objects (such as counters or cubes) to represent different animals to show where they are placed on the ark (fluency through representing numbers in a concrete way). Learners might find the work of Carl Linnaeus helpful, a scientist who identified a way to classify and name all life on Earth. His evidence may contribute to where learners decide to place the animals on the ark. For more information, visit www.nhm.ac.uk.

NC mathematics objectives

- Solve number and practical problems (Year 3, 4, 5 and 6 number – number and place value);
- Identify multiples and factors (Year 5 number – multiplication and division).

NC science objectives

- Use straightforward scientific evidence to answer questions or to support their findings (Lower Key Stage 2 working scientifically);

- Recognise that living things can be grouped in a variety of ways (Year 4 living things and their habitats);

- Describe how living things are classified into broad groups according to common observable characteristics and based on similarities and differences, including microorganisms, plants and animals (Year 6 living things and their habitats);

- Give reasons for classifying plants and animals based on specific characteristics (Year 6 living things and their habitats).

Topic: Trees

For this activity, you will need access to some trees. If your school grounds do not contain trees, why not take a trip to the local park?

Mathematics-led activity: Finding the height of trees

Although there are several different methods, here are two you could try.

1. Stand facing a tree. Imagine where the top of the tree would land if it were to fall towards you. Stand at this point, turn your back to the tree, and look through your legs. If you can see the top of the tree, you are likely to be correct. If not, adjust how near or far you are away from the tree. Now measure the distance.

2. If you have one, use a clinometer. Look at the tree and estimate its height. Use your clinometer to make an angle of 45° with the top of the tree. Measure the distance to the tree. Now measure your own height to eye level. Add these two numbers together to work out the height of the tree.

Ask learners to discuss the different methods, and draw on both their reasoning (easiest? hardest? most accurate approach?) and problem-solving skills. Discuss when we might need to know the height of trees and how the learners' mathematical skills could help solve this real-life problem. Working mathematically is central to this context, but so is working scientifically, as the following activity reveals.

NC mathematics objectives

- Solve number and practical problems (Year 3, 4, 5 and 6 number – number and place value);

- Measure, compare, add and subtract: lengths (m/cm/mm) (Year 3 measurement);

- Estimate, compare and calculate different measures (Year 4 measurement);

- Draw given angles and measure them in degrees (Year 5 geometry – properties of shapes).

Science led activity: Roots and shoots

Now learners have practised measuring the height of trees, extend this activity by investigating trees further. You could go on a leaf hunt, where you ask learners to collect as many different leaves that they can find. Back in the classroom, ask them if they can match the leaf to the tree and name it? One of the skills in working scientifically is to group, sort and classify data (in this case leaves) and use these skills to ask and answer questions.

Learners could design a poster showing the different parts of a tree (e.g. branches, leaves, flowers, seeds, bark) and discuss what trees need to stay healthy. Alternatively, learners could make a tree booklet. They could include:

- a sketch of a tree;

- different leaves and the trees they come from;

- a bark rubbing;

- different types of trees (e.g. coniferous trees);

- how trees grow;

- animals that live in or use trees;

- the uses of wood.

Why not conclude the activity by giving the learners different seeds from trees to plant and take home (e.g. acorn, sycamore seed, apple seed)?

NC science objectives

- Record findings using simple scientific language, drawings, labelled diagrams, keys, bar charts and tables (Lower Key Stage 2 working scientifically);

- Gather, record, classify and present data in a variety of ways to help in answering questions (Lower Key Stage 2 working scientifically);

- Explore the requirements of plants for life and growth (Year 3 plants);

- Give reasons for classifying plants and animals based on specific characteristics (Year 6 living things and their habitats).

Figure 2.5 Learners use different methods to determine the height of a tree

Figure 2.5 Learners use different methods to determine the height of a tree

Conclusion

This chapter has shown that working mathematically is threaded throughout the mathematics curriculum (DfE, 2013) under the umbrella of fluency, reasoning and problem solving. For teachers less confident in what working mathematically looks like or how it supports mathematics learning, working scientifically within science offers this support and connection. This chapter has shown how mathematical activities are enriched through working mathematically.

Summary of learning

In this chapter, you will have learned:

- that working mathematically underpins all of mathematics, just as working scientifically enables science;
- how fluency, reasoning and problem solving support working mathematically;
- that science activities can become valuable contexts for working mathematically.

3

Number, Place Value
and Calculation

This chapter will ensure that you:

- understand the importance that number, place value and calculation have within the science and mathematics curriculum;

- appreciate how number, place value and calculation can be used to explain and quantify the scientific world;

- understand how some numbers have mathematical properties that are both aesthetically pleasing and also crop up continuously in the natural world.

Overview

Number, place value and calculation feature throughout the mathematics curriculum, and in the latest version of the English National Curriculum (DfE, 2013) are divided predominantly into four sections:

- number – number and place value;
- number – addition and subtraction;
- number – multiplication and division;
- fractions.

Years 4 to 6 also include sections on decimal numbers, percentages, ratios and algebra.

Figure 3.1 Pencil sketch of Fibonacci (c. 1170 to c. 1240)

An example of a mathematician

Leonardo of Pisa, otherwise known as Fibonacci (Figure 3.1), a nickname he gave himself, is probably most famous for the number sequence he discovered, known today as the Fibonacci sequence:

> 1, 1, 2, 3, 5, 8, 13, 21, 34, 55, 89, 144, . . .

The sequence is created by adding the two previous terms together and was a result of a problem concerned originally with the offspring of rabbits. Today, we can find many examples in both mathematics and science where the Fibonacci numbers appear. For example, if we took the time to count the number of seed spirals in a sunflower, we would find that they add up to a Fibonacci number.

Figure 3.2 A sunflower

Connecting mathematics and science: number, place value and calculation

Although we are unlikely to use all of the mathematics we learn at school in our everyday lives, number, place value and calculation are inescapable. For this reason they might be considered the most fundamental concepts within the mathematics curriculum. Without these concepts, much of the other mathematics we engage in would be difficult and often meaningless. Can you imagine trying to understand what the weather will be like tomorrow without quantitative measures, for example, reading scales?

Science in Key Stage 1 makes use of number, place value and calculation, but as the years go by the impact of this mathematical area on science becomes more profound. Much of science, like mathematics, is about relationships. These can be described without numbers (e.g. we live in a galaxy, the Milky Way, and understand there are other planets and moons and our Sun within it), but once we have numbers we have even better ways to consider these relationships (e.g. the Sun is 93 million miles from Earth, the next nearest star, Proxima Centauri is 4.24 light years away, and the Milky Way is made up of around 100 billion stars). In this way, number, place value and calculation support the transition from qualitative judgements, such as an ice cube is melting, to more quantitative measures, such as the ice cube changed state within five minutes, and this use of number, place value and calculation enables more precision in scientific discovery.

A real-life example with mathematics and science

We each have numbers that are important to us, for example, our phone number, house number or pin number. However, there are some numbers that are important in the universe and in particular to scientific discoveries and innovations. For example, it is important we know the boiling point of water (100 degrees Celsius) or that there are 364 and one-quarter days in a year. The following are a few more significant numbers that connect mathematics and science:

- 3.14 (pi or π) is an irrational number and so cannot be expressed as a common fraction. However, fractions such as 22/7 and other rational numbers are commonly used to approximate pi. Many areas of science use pi, such as within statistics, fractals, thermodynamics, mechanics and electromagnetism.
- 0.57721 (Euler's constant) has significant application in number theory but also other engineering-related formulas and calculations.
- A Googol number is the digit 1 followed by 100 zeros. While many people today would know Googol as a search engine (spelt Google©), the number is useful when comparing other very large quantities, such as the number

of subatomic particles in the visible universe or the number of hypothetical possibilities in a chess game.

- The golden ratio (approximately 1.6180339887) is the number used to describe universally perfect proportions in sciences such as architecture and anatomy. We find the golden ratio when we divide a line into two parts so that the longer part divided by the smaller part is also equal to the whole length divided by the longer part (a/b = (a + b)/a = 1.618).

- 299,792,458 m/s is the exact value that the speed of light has been calculated as. It is a universal constant and is an exact calculation as the length of the metre is defined from this constant and the international speed for time. Using this calculation we can determine that sunlight takes about eight minutes and seventeen seconds to travel the average distance from the surface of the Sun to the Earth.

Today, we use number, place value and calculation without even considering the scientific connections. For example, doses of medicine often come in a liquid form that requires us to measure accurately (e.g. 10 ml of liquid). There are many factors that have taken this dosage into consideration but we use our knowledge of number to recognise the amount required, our knowledge of place value to measure 10 ml (and not 100 ml) and our knowledge of calculation if we only need a half dose. Behind the scenes, scientists have worked out that this dosage will help to cure us rather than make our condition worse. Our knowledge of number, place value and calculation, and our trust in science, allow us to administer the safe dose.

Key teaching points for number, place value and calculation

A numeral is a symbol that we use to represent a number. The number is the concept represented by the numerals. For example, the number 365 uses the numerals (or digits) three, six and five, but together they make the number 365. The number 365 may also be represented by objects, pictures or other numerals, such as Roman numerals.

When learners begin to count, they learn that the last number in their count (e.g. one, two, three) is also the number that represents the set as a whole. This is known as the cardinal number. Learners also encounter numbers that are used to label things in order (e.g. first, second, third). This is the ordinal aspect of number.

Mathematics is made up of different types of numbers too. Natural numbers or integers are the set of numbers we use for counting – starting one, two, three – and go on infinitely. Integers include positive and negative numbers and zero. We sometimes refer to natural numbers or integers as whole numbers. Rational numbers, in contrast, are numbers that can be written as a fraction, where the numerator and denominator are both whole numbers (excluding zero). Examples of rational numbers include 4/3, –9/2, 1.5, 1/6.

The number system we use today was originally derived from an ancient Hindu system, which was developed by Arab traders. It is known today as the Hindu-Arabic number system and uses the place a numeral is recorded in to determine the number. For example, the number 444 uses one symbol of four to represent four hundreds, four tens and four ones. We refer to this as place value. Our number system also uses ten as a base. Resources such as base-ten blocks are particularly useful in showing learners the base ten system and how we use the concept of exchange, so when we have ten ones we can exchange these for one ten.

Finally, it is important to briefly mention zero, which is used either as a place holder in our number system or to represent nothing. For example, with the number 205, zero is used to indicate the position of the tens place. The answer is also zero. While there are many who refer to zero as a number, it is more often thought of as a concept, rather than a number.

Due to limitations of space, we are unable to explore the wealth and depth of understanding surrounding calculation strategies here, so we will focus on the key aspects. For all four calculation strategies there are a variety of methods learners are taught. However, the key teaching points are not concerned with the methods but with the structures of the calculations themselves. Addition, for example, can be solved in a number of ways (e.g. combining two or more quantities together to result in a single quantity or increasing an amount by adding on a quantity). For example, we can solve addition questions by partitioning numbers and adding them together, using a number line to support adding partitions of the number, and using the commutative law to understand that the numbers can be added in any order. Subtraction, multiplication and division have their own structures that are both similar to addition but also unique in their own ways. For example, subtraction is not commutative. We can also solve calculations in a more formal way, using a set of rules (e.g. adding numbers in a column where the digits are added together, as opposed to adding numbers according to their place or quantity value).

However, recent research has demonstrated that primary age learners who have a good understanding of the place value principle are more successful than their peers who use digits in their calculations (Borthwick and Harcourt-Heath, 2015; Thompson and Bramald, 2002). Those learners who use strategies such as number lines, arrays and partitioning are more likely to reach the correct answer and understand why (Skemp, 1976), than learners who deploy a formal written algorithm such as decomposition or long multiplication or long division.

Teaching activities linking mathematics to science

Key Stage 1

Topic: The Bad-Tempered Ladybird

Activity: Making ladybirds

This activity is inspired by a book written by Eric Carle, *The Bad-Tempered Ladybird* (2010) – a ladybird that picks fights with every animal it meets, but soon learns the importance of friends. Ask learners what they think made the ladybird bad tempered. Was the ladybird hungry, lonely, tired or too hot? Provide some information cards for learners and ask them to consider possible reasons (Table 3.1). This would be a useful activity to work on in groups of four.

To begin, you could give learners some (paper) ladybirds to sort. Figure 3.3 shows ladybirds sorted by their number of spots: ladybirds with spots below five, above five and exactly five spots. This reinforces counting principles as well as other number skills.

Next, ask learners to make an alternative version of *The Bad-Tempered Ladybird*. On the underside, ask them to include a piece of information about how to make a ladybird happy. On the top, get them to design their own ladybird (Figure 3.4). Provide place value, number

Table 3.1 Ladybird information cards

What do ladybirds eat? Ladybirds are meat eaters (carnivores) and so they like to eat greenfly, small caterpillars and other invertebrates. Gardeners love ladybirds because they help to eat all the pests that eat their vegetables. A seven-spot ladybird can eat 5000 greenfly during its life.	*Do ladybirds sleep?* Ladybirds hibernate, which means they sleep through the winter. During the spring and summer months, they are active looking for food. However, ladybirds only survive for one year.
Are there different types of ladybirds? In Britain there are forty-six different types of ladybird, the most common being the seven-spot ladybird. Although there are many different types of ladybird, they usually prefer to be alone, except when they hibernate.	*Do ladybirds like hot or cold temperatures?* Ladybirds are very active in the spring and summer because they like the warm weather.

and calculation challenges to inspire the number of spots they choose to include. For example, you could ask them to make a ladybird that:

- has an odd number of spots;
- has exactly 26 spots;
- has fewer than 22 spots but more than 15 spots;
- has an even number of spots on one wing and an odd number of spots on the other;
- has the same number of spots on left and right wings;
- when multiplied together, the spots on the two wings total 24;
- is divided into four parts with each part containing one more spot than the previous part.

Remember to read the story *The Bad-Tempered Ladybird* (Carle, 2010) to the learners at some point! There are lots of other activities you can do within this topic. You could go on a ladybird hunt around school. How many ladybirds can learners spot? Are they all seven-spot ladybirds or different types? Use the UK Ladybird survey and input the data online. Investigate setting up a ladybird-friendly area in the school grounds. Make sure there are opportunities for the ladybirds to hibernate by providing a ladybird house. You could also investigate the life cycle of a ladybird.

For further information on ladybirds, you could visit the following websites:

www.hdra.org.uk/factsheets/gg12.htm

www.face-online.org.uk

www.youtube.com/watch?v=SvHWxDjfFB8

NC mathematics objectives

- Count, read and write to 100 in numerals; count in multiples of twos, fives and tens (Year 1 number and place value);
- Given a number, identify one more and one less (Year 1 number and place value);
- Recall and use addition and subtraction facts to 20 fluently, and derive and use related facts up to 100 (Year 2 addition and subtraction);

- Recall and use multiplication and division facts for the 2, 5 and 10 multiplication tables, including recognising odd and even numbers (Year 2 multiplication and division).

NC science objectives

- Gather and record data to help in answering questions (Key Stage 1 working scientifically);
- Identify and name a variety of common animals (Year 1 animals, including humans);
- Identify and name a variety of common animals that are carnivores, herbivores and omnivores (Year 1 animals, including humans);
- Identify that most living things live in habitats to which they are suited and describe how different habitats provide the basic needs of different kinds of animals and plants, and how they depend on each other (Year 2 living things and their habitats);
- Find out about and describe the basic needs of animals for survival (water, food and air) (Year 2 animals, including humans).

Teaching tip

Why not make a giant ladybird? How many spots could you mark on it?

Figure 3.3 Sorting ladybirds

Figure 3.4 Happy numbered ladybirds

Topic: Dinosaurs

Mathematics-led activity: Multilink dinosaurs

Ask learners to 'create' a dinosaur from multilink cubes (Figure 3.5). You can allocate different values to the cubes (e.g. red = 50, black = 25, blue = 10, green = 5, brown = 1). Give a total for the dinosaur (e.g. 240). Explain to learners that there are just two rules:

1. The dinosaur must be attractive (this stops learners just using one or two colours, and also makes them think about the cubes you have not given a value to);

2. The cubes must total the number you have chosen.

Ask them to prove that their finished dinosaur contains cubes to the value required, drawing on their working mathematically skills (Figure 3.6).

Try watching the 1999 'Walking with Dinosaurs' BBC television programme (available online) or visit the Smithsonian website for further ideas (www.si.edu). Another dinosaur-related activity is to ask learners to draw one to scale on the playground using chalk.

Choose several dinosaurs that are of varying sizes. Figure 3.7 shows a few examples. Using metre sticks and tape measures, ask learners to draw the dinosaurs as accurately as they can. This requires learners to read, write and calculate the numbers within a context (Figure 3.8).

Learners could also compare themselves with a dinosaur to determine who is the longest (Figure 3.9).

NC mathematics objectives

- Solve problems with addition and subtraction using concrete objects and pictorial representations (Year 2 number – addition and subtraction);
- Add and subtract numbers using concrete objects, pictorial representations, and mentally, including a two-digit number and ones, a two-digit number and tens, and two-digit numbers (Year 2 number – addition and subtraction).

Science-led activity: Dinosaur care

Ask learners to suggest how they would look after their multilink dinosaur if it was real. What would they need to provide for their dinosaur to keep it alive? Learners could even make a habitat for their dinosaur out of, for example, a shoe box. Discuss that different animals need different food sources, depending whether they are meat eaters or plant eaters. Can learners classify their dinosaurs into carnivores and herbivores and suggest animals that would fit into these categories today? What about an omnivore? Which animals would fit into this classification today?

NC science objectives

- Identify and name a variety of common animals that are carnivores, herbivores and omnivores (Year 2 animals, including humans);
- Find out about and describe the basic needs of animals (including humans) for survival (water, food, air) (Year 2 animals, including humans).

You may also find the following websites helpful:

www.nhm.ac.uk
www.enchantedlearning.com/subjects/dinosaurs
www.kids-dinosaurs.com

Teaching tip
Using the playground as a context for learning can be a very powerful way to engage learners.

Figure 3.5 Making a multilinked dinosaur

Figure 3.6 A finished dinosaur

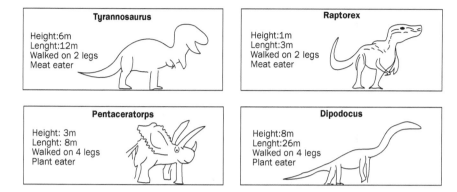

Figure 3.7 Example of dinosaurs to scale

Figure 3.8 Learners drawing their dinosaurs on the playground

Figure 3.9 Working out who is the longest, the learners or the dinosaur?

Key Stage 2

Topic: The golden ratio

Activity: Finding the golden ratio in our bodies

The golden ratio is perhaps one of the most famous numbers to both mathematics and science and so we had to include it here! It is a special number approximately equal to 1.618 and was first associated with the ancient Greeks who used it to produce the most pleasing of shapes, while the Egyptians used it in the construction of the pyramids.

The Parthenon, in the Greek capital of Athens, was constructed during the era of Greek mathematics, using the golden ratio (Figure 3.10). If we were to draw a rectangle around the Parthenon, we could calculate that it is a special rectangle. Such a rectangle can be any width, but its length has to be just over 6/10 longer than its width. Such rectangles are known as 'golden rectangles', which means that their side lengths are in the golden ratio.

In mathematics, a ratio is used to compare the sizes of two or more quantities. Two quantities are in the golden ratio if their ratio (of the longer part divided by the smaller part) is equal to the whole length divided by the longer part. Look at Figure 3.11 and the accompanying explanation if you find this tricky to understand.

This activity makes use of learners' mathematical skills to practise finding the golden ratio and knowledge of their science skills to locate the golden ratio in the dimensions of our bodies! Begin by giving learners a set of numbers, for example, 1, 1, 2, 3, 5, 8, 13, 21, 34, 55, etc. Do the learners recognise the numbers? Can they explain the pattern? Can they predict the next number in the sequence? These are the Fibonacci numbers, created by adding the two previous numbers (or terms) together. Using calculators, challenge the learners to divide each number by the one that comes before it. Challenge learners to see how many calculations they can do in twenty minutes. For example:

$1/1 = 1$
$2/1 = 2$
$3/2 = 1.5$
$5/3 = 1.666666$
$8/5 = 1.6$

What do learners notice is happening to the answer? How close can they get to 1.618? This activity helps learners to understand how important calculators are in the world of mathematics.

Once learners have practised finding the golden ratio, it is time to put it into context. We have already seen how it was used in buildings such as the Parthenon to make it look appealing. However, many mathematicians, artists and philosophers believe the golden ratio is also present in humans, to make us look attractive too! So, do our bodies use the golden ratio?

Each hand has five digits, and each digit has four parts separated by knuckles (Figure 3.12). Ask learners to look at the bones on one of the fingers, and in particular the length of the bone from the first knuckle to the second knuckle and then from the second knuckle to the third knuckle. Ask them to measure these parts, and then divide the first number by the second. What do they notice? Are they close to finding the golden ratio? What about the other two parts of the digit? Are these sections of bone also in the golden ratio?

Now get them to measure the distance from their elbow to their wrist, and then the length of their hand. Again, divide the first number by the second number and record the results. What do they notice? Perhaps the class could make a life size skeleton of one of the learners and mark where the golden ratio appears!

Later on in their scientific explorations, learners will discover how the golden ratio is used in architecture, in hurricanes and in nature, such as in DNA. This activity provides a platform for this curiosity to develop. So, the golden ratio really is one of the world's most astonishing numbers running through the heart of mathematics and science!

NC mathematics objectives

- Multiply and divide whole numbers and those involving decimals (Year 5 number – multiplication and division);
- Solve problems involving multiplication and division (Year 5 number – multiplication and division);
- Solve problems involving addition, subtraction, multiplication and division (Year 6 number – addition, subtraction, multiplication and division).

NC science objectives

- Use straightforward scientific evidence to answer questions or to support learners' findings (Upper Key Stage 2 working scientifically);
- Identify that humans and some other animals have skeletons and muscles for support, protection and movement (Year 3 animals, including humans).

Teaching tip

The golden ratio is often denoted by the Greek letter phi (Φ or ϕ). It is an irrational mathematical constant, approximately 1.6180339887.

Figure 3.10 The Parthenon, Athens

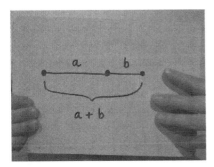

Divide the longer part (a) by the smaller part (b), and then divide the whole length (a + b) by the longer part (a). If the answers are equal then these two quantities (a and b) are in the golden ratio.

These two quantities could be the sides of a rectangle.

Here is an example to try.
Line a = 61.8 cm
Line b = 38.2 cm
61.8 cm ÷ 38.2 cm = 1.618 cm
61.8 cm + 38.2 cm = 100 cm
100 cm ÷ 61.8 cm = 1.618 cm

Figure 3.11 The golden ratio

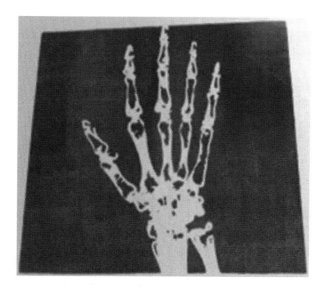

Figure 3.12 A representation of an X-ray of a human hand

Topic: Penguins

Read the book *365 Penguins* (Fromental, 2006) as a starting point to introducing this activity. On New Year's Day, a family receives a surprise present – a penguin! Every day thereafter they receive another penguin. As more penguins arrive the family need to consider how to sort them, what to feed them and also who is sending them!

Mathematics-led activity: Numicon© penguins

We have used Numicon© as the mathematical resource for this activity but you could also use cubes, Cuisenaire© rods or squared paper. Ask learners to make a penguin using Numicon© that totals in some way 100. Compare the different ways they have added the Numicon© tiles together to assemble their penguins (Figure 3.13). Next, ask learners to work out the proportion represented by each colour (Figure 3.14). Learners could calculate the fractions, decimals, percentages or ratio numbers. Remind learners to be systematic in their written jottings. Perhaps learners could convince each other that their calculations are correct. Once learners have made a penguin that totals 100, challenge them to make another penguin with a different numerical value.

NC mathematics objectives

- Recognise, find and write fractions of a discrete set of objects: unit fractions and non-unit fractions with small denominators (Year 3 fractions);

- Solve problems that require knowing percentage and decimal equivalents of ½, ¼ (Year 5 fractions, including decimals and percentages).

Science led activity: Hot or cold?

Ask learners to suggest different ways as to keep a penguin cold (Figure 3.15). Which materials are good insulators? Set up an experiment to explore which materials are good at keeping an ice cube cold. Provide learners with a variety of containers, such as Styrofoam©, foil and cotton wool. Place an ice cube inside each insulator and observe which material keeps the ice cube intact the longest (Figure 3.16). Encourage learners to ask their own questions and make decisions about how they might set up the experiment so that skills of working scientifically are developed.

NC science objectives

- Set up simple practical enquiries, comparative and fair tests (Lower Key Stage 2 working scientifically);

- Observe that some materials change state when they are heated or cooled (Year 4 states of matter).

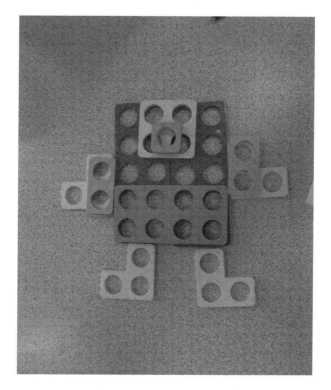

Figure 3.13 A Numicon© penguin

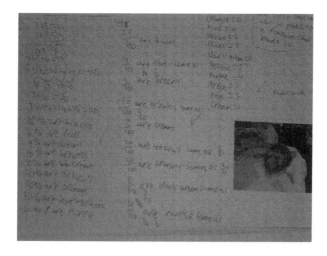

Figure 3.14 Year 5 calculating the proportionality of their Numicon© penguins

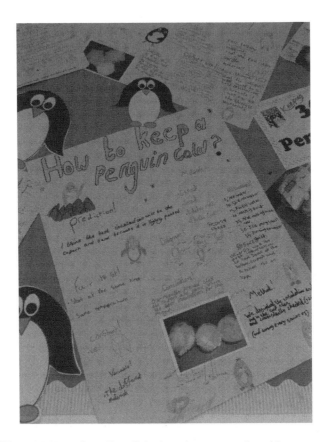

Figure 3.15 Initial ideas from Year 5 for keeping a penguin cold

Figure 3.16 Experiment to test which materials are the best insulators

Conclusion

This chapter has explored the importance of number, place value and calculation and has shown that it is essential knowledge for exploring the world of mathematics and science. We are surrounded by numbers and use them subconsciously in our mathematical and everyday lives, but also within every aspect of science.

Summary of learning

In this chapter, you will have learned:

- that number, place value and calculation have equal importance in both science and mathematics;
- that the use of quantitative measures allows pattern and relationships to be identified;
- that some of the most important mathematical discoveries around number are connected to the most important scientific discoveries we know of today.

4

Proportionality

This chapter will ensure that you:

- understand how proportionality fits into and contributes to the primary mathematics curriculum;

- recognise how proportionality is present in many scientific concepts.

Overview

Proportionality is often referred to as one of the big ideas in mathematics, as it appears in many areas of mathematics. However, it is not a word we often use in primary schools, even though as a mathematics concept it appears in every year group and Key Stage. Proportionality is concerned with the relationship between the parts of a whole and the whole itself, and between one part and another. We can describe proportionality in different ways: as fractions, decimals, percentages, proportions and ratio. We could ask what proportion of the class has blue eyes? We could answer ¼, 0.25, 25%, one in every four learners or 1:3. It is also helpful to think of proportionality as scale. The toy cars learners sometimes play with are a smaller version of real cars. For example, the scale model Formula One cars are usually made using a 1:8 scale, meaning that the toy cars are eight times smaller than the real ones.

All year groups in the latest version of the English National Curriculum (DfE, 2013) include some reference to proportionality, within, for example, fractions, decimals or percentages. Most of these objectives appear within the sections on number, but we also use proportionality in other areas of mathematics: geometry (when we compare two triangles that are similar in every way except their size), word problems (for every five degrees increase in temperature, we sell twenty-four more ice creams) and measurement (where different units are related proportionally, e.g. 100 cm = 1 m).

An example of a mathematician

Leonardo da Vinci is probably best known for his paintings, rather than as a famous mathematician (Figure 4.1). However, we have included him in this chapter because of his drawing *The Vitruvian Man*. The drawing, which depicts a man in two positions, and is inscribed within a square and circle (Figure 4.2), is based on the correlations of ideal human proportions, otherwise known as the golden ratio (see Chapter 3 for further discussion and activities on the golden ratio, and Chapter 15 on animal biology). Science, and in this example human

Figure 4.1 Pencil sketch of Leonardo da Vinci (1452–1519)

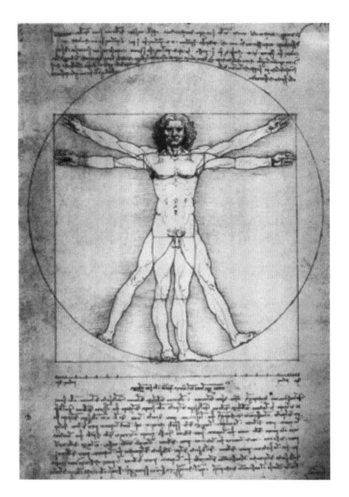

Figure 4.2 The Vitruvian Man I

biology, shows learners that proportionality does have meaning and purpose in real life, as well as in the mathematics classroom!

Connecting mathematics and science: proportionality

Combining science and mathematics to understand something like proportionality enriches and enables learners. For example, maps use a scale, in cooking we use ratios to measure out the ingredients, and engineers often make scale replicas before building life-size models. Mathematics and science have long since been connected within this area. In science or mathematics lessons, we might group learners in a class according to eye colour (20% have blue eyes), hair

(¼ have long hair) or who is left handed (one in every fifteen). The biology of human beings provides us with a rich source of data that we can express as a fraction, decimal, percentage or ratio.

A real-life example with mathematics and science

With seven books, eight films, ten years of filming, five warehouses and two aircraft hangers of props, most people have heard of Harry Potter and the magical wizarding world created by J.K. Rowling. There were several features within the films that used scale and proportionality, such as Hagrid the Gamekeeper, Professor Flitwick, the model of Hogwarts, which was used to film many of the scenes, Aragog the gigantic spider and Fluffy the three-headed dog. However, one example in particular used the knowledge and skills of both mathematics and science. In the first book, *The Philosopher's Stone* (Rowling, 1997), the three main characters have to solve a series of problems and puzzles to find the stone. One of these puzzles involves Ron participating in a life-size game of chess. This required the prop team to calculate the scale factor and proportions of each chess piece. The choice of material used to build the pieces also needed careful consideration, along with the mass of each piece so that Ron could comfortably sit astride the Knight without it collapsing.

Key teaching points for proportionality

Teaching fractions as part of a unit is often the first way learners understand and experience proportionality. The unit (often a whole) is divided up into equal parts and then certain parts are shaded. Learners calculate what fraction is shaded and what not shaded. Fractions as part of a set extend the idea of fractions as a unit to include a number of equal parts of a set, for example, finding two-thirds of 12. It is also important that learners understand that fractions represent a division calculation (e.g. ⅗ is three divided by five). Finally, fractions can be used to compare one quantity with another (which is ratio); for example, we can compare two prices of £2 and £4 by stating that one is half of the other.

There are many mathematical words associated with fractions (e.g. numerator, denominator, proper and improper, mixed numbers). It is important that learners use the correct vocabulary but also understand what the words mean.

Equivalence between fractions is a key idea within proportionality. Learners need to understand that a whole is equivalent to two halves, which is equivalent to four quarters, which is equivalent to three thirds, and so on. This helps to see patterns in fractions and allows learners to move easily between representations. This is particularly helpful when using proportionality across subjects.

Although we use fraction notation more than we use ratio in primary schools, fractions can also be expressed as ratios and this is particularly important within science (for example, in scale drawings and on maps). Learners need to understand the concept of proportionally rather than just experience fractions in their most common form (for example, ½, ⅓).

Teaching activities linking mathematics to science

Key Stage 1

Topic: Rapunzel's garden

Activity: Planning and making the garden

This activity challenges learners to plant a garden for Rapunzel. However, Rapunzel has certain criteria that must be followed. Her garden needs to include:

- colour;
- plants to eat;
- grass; and
- a surprise!

The mathematics part of this challenge is to use knowledge of fractions to ensure the whole garden is used and the proportions all total one (garden). The science aspect of this activity is to learn more about plants and flowers, including some of their names and how they grow.

Ask learners to plan their garden on paper first before planting it out in containers. They must decide how much of the garden to give each section. For example, they may decide to divide their garden into tenths or thirds. However, you could also encourage a mixture of fractions. Learners in one Year 2 class (Figure 4.3) decided to divide their garden into eighths and quarters and were very successful in planning their plants, flowers and grass. This activity encourages learners to go beyond the National Curriculum (DfE, 2013) requirements at this Key Stage but in doing so helps strengthen their understanding of proportionality.

Discuss with learners what makes a garden colourful. Explore different flowers and their names. Which flowers do the learners prefer? Rapunzel also needs to grow plants she can eat. Make a list of plants they could include, such as carrots, lettuce, cress, onions, parsley, garlic or basil.

The surprise section is for them to use their creative skills to decide what should go there. To support learners in deciding which flowers and plants to include, try, where possible, to have real-life examples. This also provides opportunities to use hand lenses to observe flowers and plants in detail, which combines important working scientifically skills. Encourage them to compare and contrast the different plants and flowers. Useful pedagogical questions include 'What is the same?' and 'What is different?'

Once learners have planned their garden on paper, plant it out in containers or in a patch of the school grounds. This allows the activity to be extended over several weeks, as learners need to discover what their seeds and bulbs require in order to grow. Finally, look at the different ways learners divided up their gardens. Chapter 16 contains further activities on observing, describing and growing plants.

NC mathematics objectives

- Recognise, find and name a half as one of two equal parts of an object, shape or quantity (Year 1 fractions);
- Recognise, find and name a quarter as one of four equal parts of an object, shape or quantity (Year 1 fractions);
- Recognise, find, name and write fractions ⅓,¼,¾ and ¾ of a length, shape, set of objects or quantity (Year 2 fractions);
- Write simple fractions for example, ½ of 6 = 3 and recognise the equivalence of ¾ and ½ (Year 2 fractions).

NC science objectives

- Identify and classify (Key Stage 1 working scientifically);
- Identify and name a variety of common wild and garden plants (Year 1 plants);
- Identify and describe the basic structure of a variety of common flowering plants, including trees (Year 1 plants);
- Observe and describe how seeds and bulbs grow into mature plants (Year 2 plants);
- Find out and describe how plants need water, light and a suitable temperature to grow and stay healthy (Year 2 plants).

Teaching tip

Many learners associate fractions with objects or quantities, rather than as a number. Take as many opportunities as possible to see fractions as numbers, for example, on a number line, and link fractions to division, so that ¾ is also expressed as three divided by four.

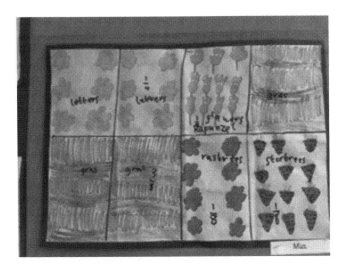

Figure 4.3 An example of Rapunzel's garden using quarters and eighths

Topic: The Iron Man

Primary learners are very interested in the human body. The proportions of the body are of real interest (see also Chapter 15). You could read either *The Iron Man* (2005a) or *The Iron Woman* (2005b) by Ted Hughes as an introduction to this activity. As the titles suggest, The Iron Man (or Woman) is a larger than life size creature, reported to be '*taller than a house*' (2005a) and so fits in very well within this mathematical area of proportionality.

Mathematics-led activity: As big as a giant or as a small as a mouse?

Use ideas from the book to challenge learners to draw their own Iron Man or Iron Woman. How much taller than them is their Iron Man or Iron Woman? Here are some suggestions (Figure 4.4):

Challenge 1: In the book, Iron Man is taller than a house. How tall is this? Can you make an Iron Man taller than a house?

Challenge 2: Choose one person in your group and make an Iron Man that is double their height.

Challenge 3: Choose one person in your group and make an Iron Man that is half their height.

Challenge 4: Choose one person in your group and make an Iron Man that is a quarter of their height.

NC mathematics objectives

- Recognise, find and name a half as one of two equal parts of an object, shape or quantity (Year 1 number – fractions);

- Recognise, find, name and write fractions ⅓,¼,²⁄₄ and ¾ of a length, shape, set of objects or quantity (Year 2 number – fractions).

Science-led activity: What makes Iron Man strong?

This activity explores the different properties of materials and considers why Iron Man was made from metal. Ask learners what might happen if Iron Man was made from a different material, say, wood, fabric, glass or jelly? Would it still be an Iron Man?

Ask learners to find objects around the classroom that are made from different materials. Can they find something that is made from wood, metal, plastic and glass? Are these materials hard or soft? Can learners find a material that is soft, for example, curtains, cushions or beanbags? Ask them to use their mathematical skills to sort the materials using simple characteristics, such as:

- hard or soft;

- bendy or rigid;

- shiny or dull.

Learners will also notice that many objects have more than one property and so could fit into more than one category. Remember, it is the material that makes the object hard or soft (for example) not the object itself, as this is often a common misconception. Chapter 14 provides more opportunities to connect science and mathematics using materials.

NC science objectives

- Identify and name a variety of everyday materials, including wood, plastic, glass, metal, water and rock (Year 1 everyday materials);

- Identify and compare the suitability of a variety of everyday materials, including wood, metal, plastic, glass, brick, rock, paper and cardboard for particular uses (Year 2 uses of everyday materials).

Teaching tip

Learners could explore scaling using a calculator. Key in two multiplied by two, then use the constant function (press the addition button twice, followed by the equals button) to produce a scale factor of two. How many presses of the 'equals' button would it take to reach 1000?

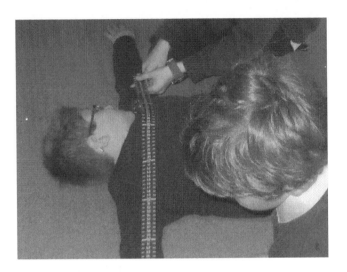

Figure 4.4 Learners calculate Iron Man proportions

Key Stage 2

Topic: Starry Night, by Vincent Van Gogh

Activity: Make a scale model of the planets in the Solar System

Introduce this activity by showing learners the short video clip 'The Powers of Ten' (you can find it at www.powersoften.com). The film begins by focusing on two people having a picnic in a park. The image starts with a scale of one metre squared. The camera then slowly zooms out to view ten metres, then one hundred metres and so on (at a rate of one power of ten per ten seconds). Finally, it zooms out into space before zooming back again. The film helps us to visualise the magnitude of scale and proportionality regarding Earth in space (Chapter 10).

Now look at the painting by Vincent van Gogh, Starry Night. What can learners see in the painting? Focus on the stars and the Moon. Figure 4.5 shows one learner's interpretation of Starry Night. Both the painting and the Powers of Ten presentation remind us of our position in space.

Tell learners they are going to make scale models of the planets in the solar system (see Figure 4.6 for an example). This activity helps them to understand and calculate the proportion of different planets in relation to the Earth and also provides a context to explore Earth and space. It is an opportunity to develop questions that lead to enquiries connecting science and mathematics.

Establish that there are eight planets and Pluto (dwarf planet). There are various methods for creating scale models of the planets (for example, creating 3-D models). One way is to use the diameters of the planets and then scale them down. The activity below is based upon Earth's diameter (7973 miles or 12,756 km) being equal to 10 cm. Table 4.1 provides the diameters of the planets. (Chapter 10 includes different ways to make models of the Solar System.)

Once complete, use the opportunity to discuss what learners know about different planets. Remember that all the planets rotate or spin on their axis but at different speeds. As learners develop their reasoning and

Table 4.1 Diameters of planets using a scale based on the Earth's diameter being equivalent to 10 cm

Planet	Actual diameter (miles)	Actual diameter (kilometres)	Model diameter (centimetres)
Mercury	3 032	4 879	3.8
Venus	7 521	12 104	9.6
Earth	7 926	12 756	10
Mars	4 222	6 794	5.4
Pluto	1 485	2 390	1.8
Jupiter	88 846	142 984	112
Saturn	74 897	120 536	94
Uranus	31 763	51 118	40
Neptune	30 775	4 928	39
Scale: Earth's diameter = 10 cm			

working scientifically skills, they should become confident in answering questions they have posed themselves. For example, where is our Moon in relation to the Earth and the other planets?

NC mathematics objectives

- Solve problems involving the relative sizes of two quantities where missing values can be found by using integer multiplication and division facts (Year 6 ratio and proportion);

- Solve problems involving similar shapes where the scale factor is known or can be found (Year 6 ratio and proportion).

NC science objectives

- Identify scientific evidence that has been used to support or refute ideas or arguments (Upper Key Stage 2 working scientifically);

- Describe the movement of the Earth, and other planets, relative to the Sun in the Solar System (Year 5 Earth and space);

- Describe the Sun, Earth and Moon as approximately spherical bodies (Year 5 Earth and space).

Figure 4.5 One learner's interpretation of Starry Night by Vincent van Gogh

Figure 4.6 Planets drawn to scale

Topic: Water

Mathematics-led activity: Memory bottles

For this activity, every learner will need their own plastic bottle, which they are going to fill with a mixture of water and oil (baby oil or cooking oils work well). You can give learners different challenges. For example:

1. Mix one part of oil to eight parts of water.

2. Mix the oil and water so they have a ratio of 1:1.

3. Mix one part of oil to every two parts of water. Have at least three parts of oil in the bottle.

4. Ensure that the bottle has 75% of water in it. How much oil is needed?

5. Mix five parts of oil to every ten parts of water.

6. If 40% of the liquid is oil, and this totals 120 mL, how much water is in the bottle?

Follow up questions could include:

- What fraction is made of water and oil?

- How many parts water are there in the mixture and how many parts oil?

- If I wanted to double or half the quantity of oil, how much water would I need to put in or take out?

For added sparkle, perhaps learners can add glitter and sequins to their bottles! When you have finished, read *Memory Bottles* (Shoshon, 2004) and ask learners to consider what memories they could 'put' inside their bottles.

NC mathematics objectives

- Solve problems that require knowing percentage and decimal equivalents of ½,¼ (Year 5 fractions – including decimals and percentages);

- Solve problems involving the calculation of percentages and the use of percentages for comparison (Year 6 ratio and proportion);

- Solve problems involving similar shapes where the scale factor is known or can be found (Year 6 ratio and proportion);

- Recall and use equivalences between simple fractions, decimals and percentages, including all contexts (Year 6 fractions – including decimals and percentages).

Science-led activity: Plasticine© boats

Challenge learners to make two Plasticine© boats, one that will float on top of the water and one that will sink. Both boats need to use the same amount of Plasticine© to make the experiment fair. Consider the shape of the boat and how this affects the density of the object. This activity allows learners to explore displacement and resistance in water (linking to the mathematics-led activity above). (See also Chapter 11 for more information on forces.)

NC science objectives

- Report and present findings from enquiries (Upper Key Stage 2 working scientifically);

- Identify the effects of water resistance that act between moving surfaces (Year 5 forces).

Conclusion

This chapter has highlighted how proportionality is present in many areas of both science and mathematics. We often use just a small piece of knowledge within this big idea but it helps us to make sense of the world around us. Both subjects are about relationships – quantitative and qualitative. As proportionality is all about relationships, it should always be in our minds as teachers planning mathematics and science.

Summary of learning

In this chapter, you will have learned:

- the key points in understanding and applying proportionality;
- the importance that proportionality plays within the mathematics curriculum and the world of science;
- that proportionality can be seen in very many contexts, ranging from Da Vinci's Vitruvian Man to planning a garden and the Solar System.

5

Pattern

This chapter will ensure that you:

- understand what is meant by pattern and where it appears in the mathematics and science curriculum;

- know how important pattern is in science and mathematics;

- understand how pattern helps to reduce confusion in science and mathematics by organising and classifying data.

Overview

Pattern is at the heart of mathematics and science. Mathematicians study and search for pattern in numbers, shape, time and space, while scientists look for patterns to make phenomena predictable. Resulting rules, laws or theorems can then be used in the world as certainties to support engineers, cooks, medical staff and pilots. Pattern is all around us. It is in the clouds above our heads, in the algorithms used by the computer within our mobile phones, and in templates used for making clothes and other artefacts. We even have our own unique patterns in our fingerprints!

Pattern does not appear, however, as a distinct section of the latest version of the English National Curriculum for mathematics (DfE, 2013), nor are there any specific objectives that use the word 'pattern'. But we need to recognise opportunities for pattern across the mathematics curriculum. Examples might include the Year 1 objective 'to count in multiples of twos, fives and tens' (Number and place value: DfE, 2013) or the Year 4 objective 'to identify lines of symmetry in 2-D shapes presented in different orientations (Geometry, properties of shape: DfE, 2013).

In science, pattern enables us to perceive and understand regularity in a seemingly chaotic world. In the past, humans saw the weather to be something caused by gods. It was Beaufort (1774–1857) who used data from weather observations to begin to provide short-term reliable weather forecasts. (For more information on Francis Beaufort, visit http://en.wikipedia.org/wiki/Francis_Beaufort.) Children can see pattern in planets, animal camouflage and the results of numerous investigations of temperature, forces and materials.

Many mathematicians consider pattern to be the most crucial and central part of learning mathematics. For example, Sawyer (1955) referred to mathematics as the classification and study of all possible patterns, while, according to Burton (1994), it is impossible to think about learning or using mathematics in any other way than by looking for patterns. Hardy (1940) believed a mathematician, like a painter or poet, is a maker of patterns. So, although pattern may not be obvious within the mathematics curriculum (DfE, 2013), it is inescapable in both the mathematics and science of our world.

An example of a mathematician

Sophie Germaine was a French mathematician, who, because she was a woman, in her early life kept her identity hidden and worked under the pseudonym of Leblanc (Figure 5.1). Even Germaine's parents were alarmed when Sophie

Figure 5.1 Pencil sketch of Sophie Germaine (1776–1831)

showed preferences in mathematics rather than cooking or dancing, believing the popular theory of the time that 'brain work' could be a dangerous strain on young girls!

Germaine is perhaps most famous for her significant contributions to number theory. In order to understand and contribute to number theory, you need to be able to look for and spot patterns within numbers. Many of the problems we solve today require us to look for patterns. Germaine used her knowledge of number theory to contribute to the mathematics of elasticity. In 1816, the French Academy awarded Germaine first prize. She was given a kilogram of gold metal worth 3000 francs, and the honour of being the first woman to receive the prestigious award. Unfortunately, most of the mathematics and science communities of the time refused to take Germaine seriously!

Connecting mathematics and science: pattern

Studying pattern is an opportunity to observe, hypothesise, experiment, discover and create. In both mathematics and science, pattern allows rules to be established (and broken). Without pattern mathematics and science would be drifting in a sea of chaotic values, measurements and clarifications.

Scientific observations of pattern in the petals of flowers revealed that many flowers follow the mathematical Fibonacci sequence (for more on Fibonacci, see Chapter 2). Just as the natural world is full of pattern (e.g. the 28 day lunar cycle and the annual cycle of 364 and a quarter days) so too, for example, is the world of statistics, where pattern helps us to predict changes over time in weather or uses of materials (when objects begin to rust, for example). Even the Solar System cannot hide from an opportunity for pattern seeking as we spot the patterns in the movement of natural bright objects in the night sky.

A real-life example with mathematics and science

Today, outbreaks of diseases such as cholera are very rare. However, in 1854, when John Snow, an English physician, looked at a map showing recent cases of an outbreak of cholera in London, his search for a pattern led him to a water well. Once he stopped people drinking water from the contaminated well, the cholera cases abated. The link was made and soon clean water supplies helped reduce occurrences of the disease and the devastation it caused. His findings resulted in fundamental changes in the water and waste systems of London, as well as in other cities, and significant improvements were made in public health. As with most scientific enquiries, Snow's initial results were not conclusive. However, his studies of the pattern of the disease were convincing enough for the local council to disable the well and, although the disease may have already been in decline, this action is credited with ending the outbreak.

Key teaching points for pattern

The problem with pattern is that there is so much to cover! Sometimes choosing what to focus on is the hardest task. Here are a few examples that are applicable to primary age learners:

- Draw learners' attention to patterns in number sequences (e.g. counting or exploring multiples and factors);
- Make connections between different areas of the mathematics and science curriculum (e.g. pattern in shape and data, Earth and Space);
- Notice that pattern begins with sorting and classifying data (e.g. sorting quadrilaterals, classifying plants and animals);
- Use learners' experiences of patterns (e.g. stretchy elastic, wallpaper, weather);
- Consider if the pattern is generalisable. Johnston-Wilder and Mason (2005) believe that 'experiencing and expressing generality is entirely natural for learners'. For example, does an odd number when added to another odd number always give an even number?
- Explore changes of state that are difficult to reverse, for example, burning or rusting;
- Explore different types of pattern: repeating pattern; radial patterns; patterns that tessellate; numeric patterns; patterns in colours, letters and sounds;
- Understand the laws of arithmetic (e.g. commutative, associate and distributive laws);
- Understand zero (e.g. zero changes depending on how it is used, so if we add zero to a number the number does not change, but if we multiply with zero the answer becomes zero);
- Know algebraic conventions.

Algebra appears as a separate section within Year 6 (DfE, 2013), although it is integral to all levels and areas of mathematics. For example, learners use knowledge of algebra when they learn about the equals sign and how this represents a balance between the two expressions either side of it. However, as learners use more complex algebraic structures, there are a few mathematical conventions to follow to avoid teaching mistakes or misconceptions:

- Don't use the same letter to represent the unknown every time;
- Remember that letters don't just stand for natural numbers, they can also be rational numbers too;
- Don't forget to use brackets if you need to;
- Avoid making incorrect generalisations such as multiplication makes numbers bigger and division makes numbers smaller;
- Don't tell learners algebra is hard, it is just an extension of number and pattern!

Due to the very nature of pattern and the need to recognise it, continue it, generate it, explain it or consider if it can be generalised, this branch of mathematics draws heavily on both working scientifically and working mathematically (the latter of which is manifested through the three aims of the latest version of the mathematics curriculum in England: DfE, 2013). In using and studying pattern, we are investigating the role and purpose of mathematics itself.

Finally, pattern allows learners to generalise in both mathematics and science, and for many mathematicians it is the core of mathematics teaching and understanding. As Johnston-Wilder and Mason (2005) write, '[a] lesson which fails to afford learners the opportunity to experience and express a generality cannot be considered to be a mathematics lesson!'

Teaching activities linking mathematics to science

Key Stage 1

Topic: Camouflage

Activity: Design repeating patterns for animal habitats

Learners find patterns aesthetically pleasing to look at. However, pattern also plays a pivotal role in the world of camouflage, helping animals to conceal themselves within their environment (such as a snowy owl's white feathers with black markings) or adding disruption, whereby the pattern breaks up their outline so it doesn't stand out against the background (such as leopards and tigers). Chapter 15 explores animal biology further.

Camouflage can be a graphical pattern and in many cases, such as in zebra, it has a repeating pattern. Begin this activity by showing learners a range of examples, say, a tiger, a cheetah, a zebra fish, a giraffe, a poisonous coral snake, a Monarch butterfly. Ask learners to explain each of the patterns to their partner. Give learners questions to address:

- Do you see a pattern?
- Is it a repeating pattern?
- Can you describe the pattern?
- Does the pattern involve colour and shape?
- Is it a regular or irregular pattern?

Investigate why animals have developed different ways to camouflage themselves throughout the course of evolution. For many animals, it is the art of not being seen, whether it be to hide from predators or to prey on others. Patterns sometimes make an animal stand out more, but they can also help to disguise them. The tiger's stripes and the giraffe's patches make them impossible to see in dappled light. The raccoon butterfly fish uses its black and yellow colouration patterns to make it hard for a predator to single out an individual in a group. The zebra's disruptive black and white stripes help to break up its outline in a herd, making it difficult for other animals, such as lions, to see it.

Usually, the pattern depends on the habitat the animal lives in and also how the animal uses the habitat – for example, if it hunts at night or lives in trees. Ask learners to look at the habitats of different animals. Can they design repeating patterns or other patterns that would allow an animal to blend in with its environment? As a class, try to cover a range of habitats (e.g. the seashore, woodland, ocean, rainforest). Once learners have finished, you might play a 'Who am I?' game. Attach the name or a picture of an animal to each learner's back. Each learner then asks probing questions to discover which animal they are.

Table 5.1 Who Am I?

Who am I?	
Do I live on land or in water?	Land.
Do I live in the open or in a tree?	In the open, but you prefer to live where there are trees and clumps of tall grass to shade you from the sun.
Is my pattern made from spots or stripes?	Stripes.
What colour am I?	Orange and black.
Am I a tiger?	Yes!

You could conclude the activity by reading Rudyard Kipling's 'How the Leopard Got His Spots' (1902). While the story is not scientifically correct, the rationale for the leopard wanting to disappear among the trees is!

This activity shows how both mathematicians and scientists use pattern to provide answers to questions. In this activity, learners explore how different patterns on animals help them survive in their own habitats. Making the link between mathematics and science here feels simple, straightforward and very natural. Pattern is an easy concept to understand but sometimes we need to open learners' mathematical and scientific eyes to recognise the pattern and its purpose.

NC mathematics objectives

- Identify and represent numbers using objects and pictorial representations (Year 1 number – number and place value);

- Describe position, direction and movement (Year 1 geometry – position and direction);

- Identify, represent and estimate numbers using different representations (Year 2 number – number and place value);

- Order and arrange combinations of mathematical objects in patterns and sequences (Year 2 geometry – position and direction).

NC science objectives

- Identify and classify (Key Stage 1 working scientifically);

- Describe and compare the structure of a variety of common animals (Year 1 animals, including humans);

- Identify and name a variety of plants and animals in their habitats, including micro-habitats (Year 2 living things and their habitats).

Topic: Spiders

Love them or fear them, spiders appear to be one of nature's cleverest creatures. Some people even believe that spiders have super powers! While all spiders produce silk, not all of them make webs. However, it is a spider's web that this activity is centred on. The silk with which a spider builds its web uses one of nature's strongest biomaterials and it is this super silk that is responsible for spiders being attributed super powers!

Mathematics-led activity: Web patterns

Most learners will have encountered a spider's web (or cobweb). The most common type of web is the orb web, so-called because of its circular shape, resembling a giant wheel. However, if you look closely you will see that it is not actually a circle, but a polygon made up from a number of sides. While the number of sides can vary from web to web, within each individual web the number of sides remains the same. For example, if the first layer has eight sides, all of the layers that follow will also have eight sides. These are clever spiders!

To begin, ask learners to work out how much silk the spider would need to spin a web. Give learners pre-drawn webs on which they need to add in the layers between the arms of the web. Do they notice a pattern? In the example shown in Figure 5.2, the learner recognised that each time she added up a layer, the answer was even. She concluded that the pattern is even because eight is an even number. An alternative activity is to give learners some pre-drawn webs and ask them to work out the total length of the webs and to try and spot a pattern between them (Figure 5.3).

Now that learners have explored spotting patterns within different spider's webs, it is time for them to make their own web. Using their knowledge of the pattern of a web, ask them to make a web from sticks and string (Figure 5.4). They could even add a spider if they want! Once learners have created their mathematical webs, why not create a giant spider's web on the playground using masking tape or chalk?

Other mathematical and scientific facts that you could explore about spiders include:

- Jumping spiders can leap 50 times their body length;
- Spiders can run up to 70 body lengths per second;
- A strand of spider silk the thickness of a pencil could stop a Boeing 747 in flight;
- Spiders can carry up to 170 times their body weight walking across a ceiling.

NC mathematics objectives

- Count in multiples of twos, fives and tens (Year 1 number – number and place value);
- Compare, describe and solve practical problems for lengths (Year 1 measurement);
- Use place value and number facts to solve problems (Year 2 number – number and place value);
- Solve simple problems in a practical context (Year 2 measurement).

Science-led activity: What eats spiders?

Learners will have already built up some knowledge about spiders through the mathematical activity, so connecting and extending the science in this area makes sense. Discuss the main reason spiders spin webs is to catch prey to eat. The usual diet for spiders is insects, although they have been observed eating other invertebrates such as millipedes, woodlice and even small frogs! Whether we love or loathe spiders, they are very helpful to us because they eat insects that can be harmful to the crops we grow. However, where do spiders sit in the food chain?

Ask learners to draw a food chain that includes a spider. We know that spiders eat insects, but ask learners to think about which animals eat spiders. How far can they go with their food chain?

Learners could draw their food chain or cut out pictures and make a hanging food chain. In Figure 5.5, learners have created a 3-D food chain using sticks and string. Finish the activity by asking what would happen if all spiders were killed or eaten? Consider how spiders fit into our world and the role they play.

NC science objectives

- Identify and name a variety of common animals (Year 1 animals, including humans);

- Find out about and describe the basic needs of animals, including humans, for survival (Year 2 animals, including humans).

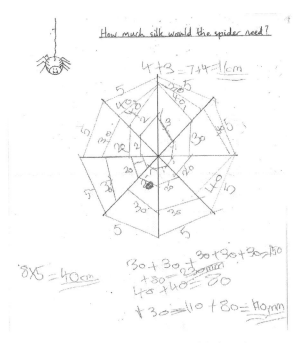

Figure 5.2 An example of pattern spotting using spider's webs

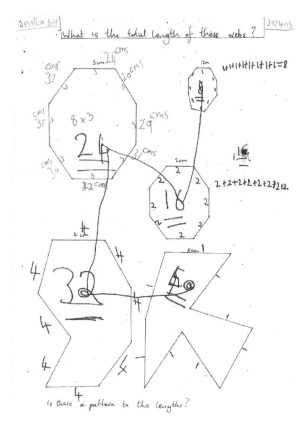

Figure 5.3 Learners look for patterns between the different lengths of webs

Figure 5.4 Learners make their own spider's webs

Figure 5.4 Learners make their own spider's webs

Figure 5.5 3D food chains

Key Stage 2

Topic: DNA

Activity: Make a DNA bead string

DNA (or deoxyribonucleic acid) is a molecule that contains genetic code, which is the blueprint for all living organisms. While learners in Key

Stage 2 are not expected to understand how genes work, this activity provides a great opportunity to link mathematics and science in a simple way (through evolution). Chapters 15 (Animal Biology) and 16 (Plant Biology) explore these areas further.

Give learners some string or cord and beads of four different colours. Ask them to cut two pieces of string, each about 30 cm long, then tie the two pieces together at one end only. Using the sequences below, ask learners to make a bracelet that carries some of the code for an organism, for example, a person, a fish, a chimpanzee or a butterfly (Table 5.2). The learners will need to work mathematically to follow the patterns and generate the sequences for the codes, while also following in the footsteps of James Watson and Francis Crick by discovering DNA.

Table 5.2 Four codes of DNA

Chimpanzee	G	T	A	T	T	T	G	T	G	G	T	A	A	A	C	C	C	A	G	T	G
Human	T	C	T	G	A	G	T	T	C	T	T	A	C	T	T	C	G	A	A	G	G
Butterfly	A	T	G	A	T	C	C	C	G	A	C	T	A	T	T	A	C	T	A	T	G
Trout	T	A	C	A	T	C	A	G	C	A	C	T	A	A	C	T	C	A	A	G	G

The codes above use four different kinds of units that make up the sequence: red, green, yellow and blue. Each bracelet contains two strands of beads that match up the same way the units in DNA do (Figure 5.6). Thus, if you know the sequence of one strand, you can work out the sequence of the other – a challenge for any future scientist or mathematician! The lines of code above are for one of the pieces of string. Learners will need to work out the sequence for the second piece of string using the following pairing rules:

DNA bases: pairing rules

A (green) pairs with T (red)

C (blue) pairs with G (yellow)

So, if they take a yellow bead and thread it onto the first piece of string, they then need to use a blue bead for the second piece of string. Once finished, the learners tie the two pieces of string together and they have their DNA bracelet (Figure 5.7).

NC mathematics objectives

- Solve number problems (Year 3, 4 and 5 number and place value);
- Generate and describe linear number sequences (Year 6 algebra).

NC science objectives

- Describe how living things are classified into broad groups according to common observable characteristics and based on similarities and differences, including microorganisms, plants and animals (Year 6 living things and their habitats);
- Recognise that living things produce offspring of the same kind, but normally offspring vary and are not identical to their parents (Year 6 evolution and inheritance).

Teaching tip

While learners may be confused and want to use the initial letter of the colour of the bead to work out the code (e.g. R for red), this is algebraically incorrect and should be discouraged.

Figure 5.6 Example of a DNA bead string

Figure 5.7 A finished DNA bead string

Topic: Symmetry

Mathematics-led activity: Digital nature books

Examples of symmetry are everywhere and this activity exploits this to connect mathematics to science. Symmetry is a type of pattern. When part of a design is repeated to make a balanced pattern, we say the design has symmetry. Artists use symmetry to make designs that are pleasing to the eye, while architects use symmetry to produce a sense of balance to their buildings. Symmetry is also present in nature.

For this activity, learners look for examples of symmetry in their outdoor environment. You might want to remind learners of the different types of symmetry that can be observed (e.g. line or reflective symmetry, rotational symmetry) or let them discover them for themselves. The following are a few examples that you could share with the learners beforehand if you wish.

Romanesco broccoli looks unusual in its appearance, but is actually one of the many examples of fractal symmetry in nature (Figure 5.8). In geometry, a fractal is a complex pattern where each part of something has the same geometric pattern as the whole. So with Romanesco broccoli, each floret has the same logarithmic spiral as the whole head (just a miniature version!).

Honeycombs are another example of symmetrical patterns in nature. Bees instinctively create hexagonal figures in honeycombs to the precision that we can only produce with a ruler and a pair of compasses! The honeycomb is a repeated pattern of near perfect hexagons.

Sunflowers also boast numerical symmetry (known as the Fibonacci sequence, see Chapter 3). So it would appear that many plants and objects in nature abide by mathematical rules. Many scientists believe it is all a matter of efficiency. For example, the hexagon is the perfect shape to allow bees to store the largest possible amount of honey, while using the least amount of wax. Other shapes, such as circles, would leave gaps, as they do not fit together exactly.

Equip learners with a camera and ask them to find and digitally record examples of symmetrical patterns in nature. Back in the classroom they can show their photographs to the class and compare their symmetrical discoveries. They could also print out their photographs and create a symmetrical collage, similar to that in Figure 5.9. However, be warned: once you have shown learners the patterns that exist in nature, they will have an uncontrollable urge to find them everywhere!

NC mathematics objectives

- Identify lines of symmetry in 2-D shapes presented in different orientations (Year 4 geometry – properties of shapes);

- Complete a simple symmetric figure with respect to a specific line of symmetry (Year 4 geometry – properties of shapes).

Science-led activity: Sugar crystals

Symmetry and pattern are so integral to the way the universe works that Albert Einstein used it as his guiding principle when he devised his General Theory of Relativity. Einstein believed that the laws of physics should be the same, regardless of how an object is moving. He discovered that physical laws act the same regardless of whether an object is accelerating or at rest. In other words, the force of gravity and the force resulting from acceleration are two aspects of the same force – that is, they are symmetrical!

There are other examples where symmetry appears in science. For example, most snowflakes consist of six arms with identical patterns on each of them, showing radial symmetry. Scientists can show how water molecules arrange themselves as they solidify, by forming weak hydrogen bonds with each other. These bonds align in an ordered arrangement that maximises attractive forces and reduces repulsive ones. This results in the overall hexagonal shape of the snowflake.

For this activity, challenge learners to make crystal rocks. A crystal refers to any matter that is arranged in an ordered form, or pattern. There are many different types of crystals you can grow, but sugar crystals are a great introduction. To grow your crystals you will need: a bowl of warm water and some sugar; a jam jar, pencil and string; and food colouring.

Tie the string to the pencil so that the string hangs into the jar without touching the sides or the bottom. Add lots of sugar (the solute) into the pan of warm water (the solution) but not so much that it doesn't all dissolve. If you have some un-dissolved sugar, your rock crystals will start to build here rather than on your string. At this point you might want to add some food colouring to the solution. Finally, pour the solution into the jar and let the crystals form (Figure 5.10). This might take up to a week. Once they have stopped growing, taste them! Explore any symmetrical patterns that emerge. You could always examine the crystals using hand lenses, to try and spot the patterns within the tiny particles.

NC science objectives

- Report findings from enquiries, including oral and written explanations, displays or presentations of results and conclusions (Lower Key Stage 2 working scientifically);

- Compare and group together different kinds of rocks on the basis of their appearance and simple physical properties (Year 3 rocks).

Figure 5.8 Romanesco broccoli Image taken form Wikimedia Commons

Figure 5.9 A butterfly collage to show symmetrical patterns in nature

Figure 5.10 An example of a sugar crystal

Conclusion

This chapter has considered what we mean by pattern in the world and how important it is to science and mathematics. It is hard to imagine teaching these subjects without mentioning pattern. At times pattern can be straightforward and simple, but it can also be complex and intriguing. This is what makes learning about pattern so interesting and relevant to both the world of mathematics and of science.

Summary of learning

In this chapter, you will have learned:

- the different ways pattern is present in mathematics and science;
- that pattern is intrinsic to both science and mathematics;
- that pattern helps us to make sense by organising and classifying experiences and data, by recognising order in the natural world.

6

Measurement

This chapter will ensure that you:

- have a good understanding of measurement as part of mathematics and science;
- understand how measurement offers many opportunities to connect science to mathematics.

Overview

Measurement links number concepts to the application and use of mathematics in a variety of ways. It is often viewed as an extension of number, although mathematicians are clear about the difference between number and measurement. Whereas number can be an abstract concept, by contrast measures, as Williams and Shuard (1994) note, 'always refer to real situations'. Measurement provides a context to work scientifically and mathematically. As has been mentioned in science (see Chapter 9, Working Scientifically), learners need to work quantitatively and so numbers are needed and many are found through measurement. Science really does help mathematics here, as in science we measure a range of things from distance to forces. These measurements help us to recognise and identify patterns (Chapter 5) and then be able to extrapolate and interpret data (Chapter 8).

An example of a mathematician

Pythagoras of Samos made many influential contributions to philosophy, religion and mathematics (Figure 6.1). However, he is probably best known for

Figure 6.1 Pencil sketch of Pythagoras (c. 570 to c. 495 BC)

discovering the Pythagorean theorem: a theorem in geometry that states that in a right angled triangle the sum of the square on the hypotenuse is equal to the sum of the squares on the other two sides (Figure 6.2). While the theorem forms the basis of trigonometry, many of the fundamental principles are taught at primary

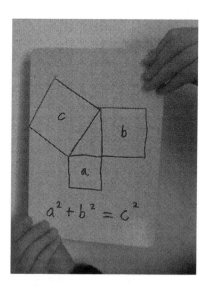

Figure 6.2 The Pythagorean theorem

school. For example, young learners love to study the different triangles and their properties, while older learners explore square numbers, key components in using Pythagoras' equation!

The Pythagorean theorem is used today in industries such as construction, engineering, architecture, design and art, and aeronautics as well as many day-to-day activities (e.g. working out how big a television you can buy depends on the diameter of the diagonal length of the screen you can fit in the space at home).

Visual representations also assist learning of concepts in mathematics and science. For example, one video clip shows a great example of why the square of the hypotenuse is equal to the sum of the squares on the other two sides, using a water-proof example! Find it at http://www.youtube.com/watch?v=hbhh-9edn3c.

Connecting mathematics and science: measurement

Learners should develop their measurement skills through practical, purposeful activities. However, it is an area of mathematics that can create difficulties because of the precise way measurements are recorded, such as to the nearest centimetre or gram. While an object will have an exact measurement, measurement itself can only be an approximation. As we often think of mathematics as an exact science, this area of mathematics often causes conflict with this concept! This is further compounded in primary classrooms where, because of inaccurate equipment, accurate measurements can be difficult or impossible to make.

Cockcroft (1982) encouraged teachers to consider all forms of measurement to be inexact and to have certain limitations. The idea that learners should be encouraged to consider the concept of 'between-ness' (DES, 1979) is still upheld as an important mathematical concept; for example, the bowl holds more than 200 grams but less than 300 grams. In this way, questions lead to how exact we want the measurements to be and the need for subdivisions. Science provides meaningful contexts to illustrate these points.

A real-life example with mathematics and science

Altogether, 196 cyclists from 74 nations participated at the 2012 London Olympics. But the team that dominated the headlines and the medal tables was the Great Britain team, attributing much of their success to mathematics and science. See Figure 6.3 for one learner's painting of a cyclist.

Cyclists use lots of different types of measurements to assess and enhance their performance. Computers are used to measure time, distance, speed, cadence, elevation and heart rate to establish how well a cyclist is performing and whether they could do any better. Measurements are taken to gauge the force the rider needs to exert on the pedals, the effect of the force of air resistance, the shape of the helmet and even what the athlete needs to eat to store enough energy for the

Figure 6.3 A learner's painting of a cyclist

race. All of these details require an understanding of the units and measurements needed, in order to apply the scientific understanding. Thus, it seems that much of the success of the British cyclists was a result of connecting mathematics and science.

Key teaching points for measurement

Direct comparison is one of the key principles in understanding measurement. In other words, putting two (or more) objects in order and then comparing them. For example, we could compare which object is longer or heavier, which container holds the least or which task takes the shortest amount of time. At this stage, no units are involved. Often the mathematical symbols of greater than (>), less than (<), equal to (=) and the inequalities sign ($\neq$) are used.

Transitivity allows us to order a set of two or more objects. For example, if we know that A is longer than B and B is longer than C, then A must be longer than C. Conservation occurs in both number and measurement. It is the concept that once something has been measured or weighed, this length or mass remains unchanged even if it is moved. Conservation of length (e.g. measuring a length of wood) and conservation of mass (e.g. re-arranging a lump of clay into different smaller pieces while realising it still has the same mass) are often more easily understood than conservation of liquid volume. Here learners often find it hard to accept that the liquid in a short, wide container can still be the same amount of liquid that once occupied a tall, thin bottle.

Figure 6.4 The 'estimated' symbol

Non-standard and standard units provide the units in which to measure. Learners start by exploring non-standard units, using objects such as their hands, pencils and skipping ropes. However, learners soon realise that using non-standard units produces unreliable results and so the need to use the same standardised unit is offered. To begin with, this can be in the form of uniform non-standard units such as multilink cubes or Cuisenaire© rods. Eventually, learners will move onto using standard units such as centimetres, grams and minutes. Chapter 9 (Working Scientifically) explores SI units further, particularly as science allows the use of a wider range of measures (e.g. when measuring light or force).

All measurements are approximate. When we measure, weigh or time something, we are measuring to the nearest something. This might be to the nearest centimetre, second or gram, but it is still an approximation. We see many real-life examples of this on food and drink packages in the form of a large 'e' (Figure 6.4). This is the European symbol to show that the stated measurement is only an approximation. While the bottle of wine may indicate it contains 750 ml, it is actually between 748.5 ml and 751.5 ml.

Teaching activities linking mathematics to science

Key Stage 1

Topic: Ice

Activity: Melting ice cubes

This activity uses ice cubes to help learners explore the concept of time, while also investigating the properties of ice. Learners often find time a hard concept to grasp. That's not surprising, as statements such as 'just a minute' and 'give me a second' are not mathematically true, but we use them frequently!

To begin, ask learners how long they think it will take for an ice cube to melt. Record the range of their suggestions. Did any of them consider the environmental conditions? For example, will it take longer for the ice cube to melt on the table, on the radiator or in the cupboard? Try this comparative experiment as a whole class first, using an ice cube in a plastic tray within the normal classroom conditions. Start a one-minute timer and find out how many learners think the ice cube will melt in that time (Figure 6.5).

Repeat the experiment in groups. Remind learners to record the time the ice cubes take to melt. Vary the activity by placing ice cubes around the school to investigate the hottest and coldest parts of the building and the time it takes the ice cubes to melt. Alternatively, ask learners to collect some natural objects from outside (e.g. leaves, bark, twigs) and then freeze these objects (Figure 6.6). This time when the ice melts, the learners can investigate if the objects have changed in any way as a result of being frozen.

While the science National Curriculum (DfE, 2013) does not formally introduce 'states of matter' until Year 4, this activity helps to provide some of the knowledge needed about different materials (Chapter 14) and how they can change under certain conditions, while linking this area with time.

NC mathematics objectives

- Measure and begin to record the following: time (hours, minutes, seconds) (Year 1 measurement);
- Compare and sequence intervals of time (Year 2 measurement).

NC science objectives

- Gather and record data to help in answering questions (Key Stage 1 working scientifically);
- Describe the simple physical properties of a variety of everyday materials (Year 1 everyday materials).

Figure 6.5 A one-minute timer

Figure 6.6 A collection of nature's objects frozen in ice

Topic: Tomatoes

Mathematics-led activity: Measuring tomatoes

In preparation for this activity, try to get hold of tomatoes of different sizes. To begin, ask learners to sort them. They might do this, for example, according to colour, size (height or diameter), how spherical they are, or how many seeds they think they contain. (See also Chapter 16: Plant Biology.)

Set learners a series of challenges to measure the tomatoes in a variety of ways. To encourage them to be as creative and inventive as possible in calculating the measurements, provide them with a range of measuring equipment (Figure 6.7). For example:

- tape measure;

- rulers;

- cubes;

- string;

- scales.

Challenge learners to find as many different measurements for the tomatoes. Here are a few suggestions:

Challenge 1: How tall is the tomato?
Challenge 2: How heavy is the tomato?
Challenge 3: How 'round' is the tomato?
Challenge 4: How wide is the tomato?

Within each challenge, ask learners to order the tomatoes using the mathematical symbols >, < and = (Figure 6.8).

NC mathematics objectives

- Compare, describe and solve practical problems for lengths and heights, mass/weight, capacity and volume (Year 1 measurement);

- Measure and begin to record the following: lengths and heights, mass/weight, capacity and volume (Year 1 measurement);

- Compare and order lengths, mass, volume/capacity and record the results using >, < and = (Year 2 measurement).

Teaching tip

As a teacher, you should be clear that in classroom mathematics we are almost always measuring mass (not weight). Mass measures the amount of stuff in an object and our scales are calibrated to work on our home planet, Earth. We tend to misuse the term weight, which strictly should be measured in Newtons and which would vary if you were on a different body in space (e.g. on Earth a child might weigh 60 N but on the Moon they would weigh one-sixth of that, 10 N. Don't be surprised if you need to re-read this or think about it – you won't be the first. It might help to look at one or both of the following websites:

www.howthingsfly.si.edu

http://www.mathsisfun.com/

Teaching tip

Remember that capacity and volume both measure the size of a three-dimensional space and use the same units. However, capacity refers to the room available within the object, whereas volume is the space actually occupied by an object or substance.

Science-led activity: The life cycle of a tomato

Discuss the life cycle of a tomato with learners and then ask them to draw the different stages. (See also Chapter 16: Plant Biology.) It might look something like that in Figure 6.9: seed, young plant, mature plant, flower, fruit – on a pizza or in a salad!

NC science objectives

- Identify and describe the basic structure of a variety of common flowering plants (Year 1 plants);

- Observe changes across the four seasons (Year 1 seasonal changes);

- Observe and describe how seeds and bulbs grow into mature plants (Year 2 plants).

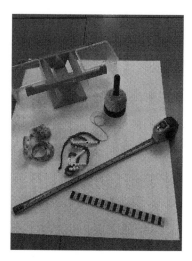

Figure 6.7 Examples of measuring equipment

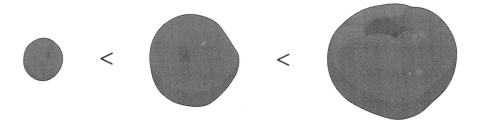

Figure 6.8 Tomatoes ordered according to size

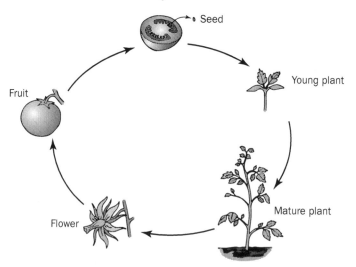

Figure 6.9 The life cycle of a tomato

Key Stage 2

Topic: Growing

Activity: Planting tomatoes

Using a real-life context such as 'growing' offers learners the opportunity to measure plants more than once, which helps to refine their measuring skills and also gives rise to plenty of situations to discuss if all measurements are fair or accurate. It also provides plenty of discussion around what plants need in order to grow. However, it also means that this activity cannot take place in just one lesson but will require several weeks to complete.

The growth of plants usually leads to very useful growth graphs. Of course, the plants are almost the living graph. Discuss with learners where to measure the height of the plants from, ensuring that whether they start at the base of the plant pot or where the plant begins to grow on top of the soil, future measurements are always taken from the same place (Figure 6.10). At each measurement, ask learners to make a Plasticine© model of the seedling. Begin by asking learners to design their own data collection sheet (Figure 6.11).

Think about placing the tomato plants in different areas of the classroom, such as on the windowsill, under the sink, in the cupboard. Discuss the conditions plants need in which to grow. Which plants grow the quickest? Which are the most healthy? Which need the most water? You could ask learners to write a list of the things plants need to survive. (For further information, see Chapter 16: Plant Biology.)

Learners could also convert the number of days the plants take to grow into hours, minutes and even seconds. Next time they are in the supermarket buying their vegetables, ask them to consider how long it took to grow each carrot, tomato, potato, and so on. Once the tomato plants start to grow, ask learners to identify the three main parts of the plants: the leaves, the stem and the roots. Ask learners to draw and label each part and provide an explanation as to the purpose of each part. You could continue this activity by going on a plant walk around the school to explore the types of plants in the immediate environment. Can learners name them all? Perhaps they could invent their own names for them. Can they distinguish between things that are alive and things that have never been alive? (For more information on plants, see Chapter 16: Plant Biology.)

NC mathematics objectives

- Measure, compare, add and subtract lengths (m, cm, mm); volume/capacity (l/ml) (Year 3 measurement);
- Solve problems involving converting from hours to minutes, minutes to seconds (Year 4 measurement).

NC science objectives

- Set up simple practical enquiries, comparative and fair tests (Lower Key Stage 2 working scientifically);
- Make systematic and careful observations and, where appropriate, take accurate measurements using standard units (Lower Key Stage 2 working scientifically);
- Explore the requirements of plants for life and growth (air, light, water, nutrients from soil and room to grow) (Year 3 plants);
- Identify and describe the functions of different parts of flowering plants: roots, stem/trunk, leaves and flowers (Year 3 plants).

Teaching tip
Check learners have included light, water, air, space, warmth and nutrients.

Figure 6.10 Measuring the height of a tomato plant

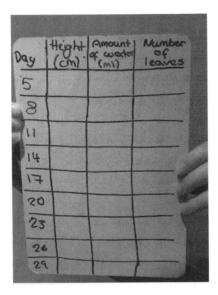

Figure 6.11 Example of a data collection sheet to measure a tomato plant

Figure 6.12 The Angel of the North Image taken form Wikimedia Commons

Topic: The Angel of the North

Designed by Antony Gormley, the Angel of the North is a steel sculpture depicting an angel, which stands twenty metres tall and has a wingspan of fifty-four metres across. It is located in Gateshead, Tyne and Wear, England (Figure 6.12).

Mathematics-led activity: Are you a square or an oblong?

Organise learners into pairs or small groups. You will need some strips of paper for this activity (till rolls work really well). Ask learners to find out if they are a square or an oblong by measuring their arm span and height (Figure 6.13). Most adults arm span is equivalent to their height, thus making them a square – that is, (i) height and (ii) fingertip to fingertip would fit inside a square – but as learners are still growing, this may not be the case, resulting in them being an oblong! Once learners have their strips of paper, measure these using tape measures or metre sticks to find out their metric units. This activity can be extended to measure different body parts. Challenge learners to discover if any other parts of the body have a ratio of 1:1. Using the Angel of the North activity, ask learners to find out how many heads fit into their body. Are they in proportion? (See Chapter 15: Animal Biology.)

NC mathematics objectives

- Measure, compare, add and subtract lengths (m, cm, mm) (Year 3 measurement);

- Convert between different units of measurement (e.g. centimetres and metres) (Year 5 measurement).

Science-led activity: Skeletons

Ask learners to find out about the human skeleton and why we need it. Essentially, there are three reasons we need a skeleton: to provide support and shape, to allow us to move using joints and to protect our internal organs. Learners might consider what would happen if we did not have a skeleton or if parts of the body were not in the proportions they currently are, or we even had new body parts (e.g. wings) like the

Angel of the North statue. Ask learners to research and know names and locations of the major bones (e.g. skull, ribs, backbone and pelvis).

Older learners could research how the human body has changed over time and find out about the work of Charles Darwin and his theory of evolution. They could consider that while we are all similar, characteristics can be passed from parents to their children, so that some of us, for example, have longer legs or shorter bodies than others. (Chapter 15 explores Animal Biology further.)

NC science objectives

- Identify that humans and some other animals have skeletons and muscles for support, protection and movement (Year 3 animals, including humans);

- Identify how animals and plants are adapted to suit their environment in different ways and that adaptation may lead to evolution (Year 6 evolution and inheritance).

Figure 6.13 Learners investigate whether they are a square or an oblong!

Conclusion

This chapter has shown how both mathematics and science rely on measurement and how the two subjects are enhanced by real-life contexts and their integration. It has emphasised the importance of measurement in science and that all measurements are only approximations.

Summary of learning

In this chapter, you will have learned:

- the key points in teaching measurement;
- there are a range of activities where mathematics and science work together to provide learners with a meaningful context;
- the value of quantitative measures to both subjects.

7

Geometry

This chapter will ensure that you:

- have a good understanding of position and direction and properties of shapes within geometry;

- explore the connections that geometry offers between mathematics and science.

Overview

Geometry is the study of shapes, sizes, positions and patterns. The latest version of the English National Curriculum (DfE, 2013) includes two strands within it: (1) position and direction and (2) properties of shape. These two strands cover classifying shapes, transformations, symmetry, coordinates and angle. The strand on properties of shape includes objectives for all year groups, whereas the strand on position and direction includes objectives for Year 1 to Year 2 and then Year 4 to Year 6.

However, the geometry we learn in school mathematics is only a fraction of the geometry we are exposed to in our everyday lives. Assembling flat packed furniture, reading maps or taking photographs all require us to think geometrically. Science provides real-life situations for us to develop our thinking in geometry.

An example of a mathematician

Many mathematicians have influenced the field of geometry (e.g. Archimedes, Descartes, Euler, Gauss, Plato), but we have chosen to focus on

Figure 7.1 Pencil sketch of Euclid of Alexandria (c. 330 to c. 275 BC)

the mathematician often referred to as the 'Father of Geometry', Euclid of Alexandria (Figure 7.1) Euclid was a Greek mathematician who is most famous for his book *Elements* (Heath, 2014), which dealt with algebra, number theory and geometry. It is reported that the book was so influential that it became the primary mathematical text for the next 2000 years! While many of the ideas in the book were not new, Euclid managed to compile all existing mathematical knowledge into a clear, uniform pattern. It is thought that no other book, other than the Bible, has been translated, edited or studied more than Euclid's *Elements*.

Euclid is responsible for five basic geometric principles:

- a straight line may be drawn from any point to point (line segment);
- a straight line may be continued infinitely in either direction;
- a circle may be drawn with any centre and radius;
- all right angles equal one another;
- if a straight line falling on two straight lines makes the interior angles on the same side less than two right angles, the two straight lines, if produced indefinitely, meet on that side on which are the angles less than the two right angles.

Figure 7.2 Casa Mila, Barcelona

The last principle is slightly harder to understand than the rest, but it basically means that lines that are not parallel will eventually meet if extended!

Connecting mathematics and science: geometry

We live in a geometric world. Everywhere we look we can see examples of squares, rectangles, triangles, parallelograms, etc. However, there is a difference between geometry in the world and mathematical geometry. If we look at the natural world, we are unlikely to see perfectly formed geometric shapes in leaves or flowers. However, having an understanding of the mathematical names for these shapes allows us to recognise and describe shapes that are recognisable even when they are not mathematically perfect. Science uses shapes in a much more fluid and organic way. For example, if you consider Gaudi's Casa Batlló and Casa Mila in Barcelona (Figure 7.2), you can see recognisable shapes in these buildings, which would not conform to any mathematical definitions! While mathematics provides the knowledge and understanding for geometry, science uses this information in a real-life, purposeful way.

Figure 7.3 The Great Pyramid of Giza

A real-life example with mathematics and science

There are many beautiful and interesting buildings around the world. Indeed, most cities can boast a famous building or two! For example, Paris has the Eiffel Tower, Barcelona hosts the Sagrada Familia Cathedral and Sydney has its Opera House. These buildings are mathematical talking points because of their shapes and the way they use geometry in their designs.

Although these buildings contain many mathematical geometric designs within them, science (e.g. materials and forces) has allowed architects to build ground-breaking structures. The link between mathematics and science in the construction industry goes back to ancient times. Some of the earliest examples include the pyramids and temples in Egypt. Using a square-based pyramid as its design, the Great Pyramid of Giza (also known as the Pyramid of Khufu) was the tallest man-made structure in the world for over 3800 years (before the spire of Lincoln Cathedral surpassed it in 1300). Now one of the Seven Wonders of the World, the Great Pyramid of Giza still remains largely intact due to the mathematical design employed and the physics used to inform its design (Figure 7.3).

Today, the geometrical designs chosen for buildings are both exciting as well as practical in their purpose. The Eden Project building in Cornwall, England, used triangles, pentagons, hexagons and other polygons in its famous greenhouse. Its design is remarkable because while none of the individual shapes are curved, when placed together they form a rounded structure, leaving the geodesic dome incredibly strong and also adaptable in that it can be built on almost any ground surface. This allowed the Eden designers to build the giant greenhouse on sloping ground in a position perfectly situated to absorb maximum light.

Key teaching points for geometry

Mathematical vocabulary is important in all strands of mathematics, but it is perhaps most prominent in geometry due to the number of words we use that also have an everyday meaning. Words such as face, side and plane, for example, are used in both everyday contexts but also in mathematics.

Invariance is a key teaching point and refers to the idea that just because a shape is presented in a different way (e.g. an upside-down triangle), it is still the same shape; in other words, it has not changed. Geometric shapes are said to be congruent if they are the same in shape and size. Learners can prove shapes are congruent by cutting them out and placing them on top of one another. Shapes can also be transformed through being translated, rotated or reflected. A translation is described by the direction and distance the shape has moved in. Rotation is a circular movement of an object or shape around a centre or point of rotation. A reflection is a transformation where the shape has been 'flipped' over the line of reflection. Every point in the new shape is the same distance from the central line and the reflection is the same size as the original image. To specify a reflection, you have to identify the mirror line.

Angle and symmetry are two more key ideas within geometry. An angle is a measure of turn and is made when two straight lines cross or meet each other at a point. The space between the lines is referred to as the angle. Symmetry of shapes or objects describes how parts of the shape or object correspond or match other parts in some way. There are three types of symmetry: line, rotational and plane.

Pierre van Hiele and Dina van Hiele-Geldof are well known for their research into the development of geometric learning, which has resulted in van Hiele's (1999) five levels of geometric reasoning. The first three are relevant to the primary age range and begin with visualisation, which is a key skill in which learners can name and recognise shapes by their appearance. The second focuses on analysis where learners begin to identify properties of shapes, and in particular use specific vocabulary related to properties. And the third is informal deduction, where learners are able to recognise the relationships between shapes and their properties.

Teaching activities linking mathematics to science

Key Stage 1

Topic: Experimenting with paper

Activity: Does the shape of a piece of paper affect how it falls?

This activity presents learners with a problem to solve. It draws on their mathematical knowledge of 2-D shapes and their scientific knowledge of materials (Chapter 14) and forces (Chapter 11).

Ask learners to design an experiment to observe how different pieces of paper fall through the air. Discuss what they could investigate, for example:

- Will the shape of the paper make a difference to the speed of descent?
- Will the number of sides make it fall faster or slower?
- Will it make a difference if the shape is symmetrical or asymmetrical?
- Will the size of the shape affect how it falls?
- Will it make a difference to the speed of descent if the paper is thick or thin?
- How can we measure the time it takes for the paper to fall?
- Which materials could we use to make the same shape fall more quickly and more slowly?

Remember to discuss how to make the test fair (e.g. dropping paper from the same height each time). Ask learners to use stopwatches to measure the speed of the shapes. While this experiment is potentially challenging, as there are many variables involved, it works well as an individual or comparative test. If learners need to gain height from which to conduct their experiment (e.g. by standing on a table as demonstrated in Figure 7.4), ensure they are aware of how to do this safely!

Learners can be given pieces of paper that are already cut into different 2-D shapes (e.g. circles, squares, oblongs, triangles, hexagons). However, a different approach is to ask learners to make their own shapes. Both approaches are worthwhile and strongly support mathematical knowledge of shapes and their properties.

Remind learners to record their findings as they go along. At the end of the experiment, discuss which pieces of paper dropped the fastest, the slowest, in a straight line or at an angle. Ask learners why certain shapes fell faster or slower and ask them to make a conjecture (Figure 7.5). For example:

- The more sides a shape has the ... it falls.
- The thicker the piece of paper the ... it falls.
- The thickness of the paper makes the shape fall ...
- Shapes with straight sides fall ...

Finally, show learners a picture of an open parachute. Ask them to imagine the parachute filling with air and explain that air resistance is a force that slows down objects. Explain that the air is pushing against the canopy and slowing it down. In theory, in the example above, larger circles should have fallen the slowest because they have the largest surface area and therefore more air resistance, so their conclusion (in Figure 7.5) provides an interesting discussion!

NC mathematics objectives

- Recognise and name common 2-D shapes (Year 1 geometry – properties of shape);
- Describe position, direction and movement (Year 1 geometry – position and direction);
- Identify and describe the properties of 2-D shapes, including the number of sides and line symmetry in a vertical line (Year 2 geometry – properties of shape);
- Use mathematical vocabulary to describe position, direction and movement (Year 2 geometry – position and direction).

NC science objectives

- Perform simple tests (Key Stage 1 working scientifically);
- Gather and record data to help in answering questions (Key Stage 1 working scientifically);
- Describe the simple physical properties of a variety of everyday materials (Year 1 everyday materials).

Figure 7.4 Learners testing whether the size of a disc affects the speed at which it falls

Figure 7.5 One hypothesis about the size of circles

Topic: Shapes in nature

Mathematics-led activity: Shape hunt

Take learners on a nature walk around the school grounds. Ask them to collect different shaped objects (e.g. leaves, rocks, feathers, pine cones and shells). Depending on how rich your natural environment is, you may need to resource it with some of these objects! Once the learners have a selection, ask them to sort according to their shape properties. Encourage them to use both 2-D and 3-D properties if possible (e.g. this may be tricky with petals). This activity gives learners opportunities to identify geometric shapes found in nature and to sort and classify objects based on mathematical attributes.

Many of the objects will not conform exactly to mathematical properties. For example, is a feather really a triangle, and if so, which type of triangle (e.g. equilateral, isosceles, scalene)? However, this activity reminds learners that the language of mathematics helps us to describe the world around us. It can also strengthen understanding of properties of shape, as we can ask questions such as 'what is the same and what is different between the feather and a triangle from the mathematics cupboard?' Figure 7.6 shows one group's hoard after just ten minutes of their nature hunt.

An alternative activity is to ask learners to find a specific number of objects (Figure 7.7). For example:

- Can you find one stone?
- Can you find two feathers?
- Can you find three leaves?
- Can you find a flower that has two different shapes in it?
- Can you find an object that has only straight edges?

NC mathematics objectives

- Recognise and name common 2-D and 3-D shapes (Year 1 geometry – properties of shape);
- Compare and sort common 2-D and 3-D shapes and everyday objects (Year 2 geometry – properties of shape).

Figure 7.6 Treasure from a shape hunt

Figure 7.7 Shapes in nature

Science-led activity: Nature detectives

With a collection of natural objects, find out the names of the flowers and leaves that learners have collected. Can they name them all? Link back to the mathematics activity and find out which shapes are missing in the nature collection. Challenge learners over the next week to try and find a hexagon or square within the natural environment. Extend the activity by asking learners to sort the objects into whether they are living, dead or inanimate (i.e. never alive). Use hand lenses to observe details to help identify and record features.

NC science objectives

- Identify and name a variety of common wild and garden plants, including deciduous and evergreen trees (Year 1 plants);

- Identify and describe the basic structure of a variety of common flowering plants, including trees (Year 1 plants);

- Identify and name a variety of plant in their habitats (Year 2 living things and their habitats).

Key Stage 2

Topic: How tough is your tetrahedron?

Activity: Testing tetrahedrons

For this activity, learners utilize their mathematical knowledge of properties of shapes and their scientific knowledge of materials. Ask learners to make a skeletal tetrahedron by rolling a sheet of A4 paper around a doweling rod to make a narrow tube. Use a hole punch to make a hole in each end, and then join them together to make a skeletal tetrahedron. How strong is the paper? Challenge learners to hang weights from the apex (Figure 7.8). Do they think it will buckle? Have a go! Try another and another, what is the class record? (See Chapter 11 for further activities on forces.)

Discuss the advantages and disadvantages of using paper as the material for the tetrahedron. Compare other properties of materials and consider which material would make the tetrahedron stronger or weaker. Perhaps challenge learners to make different tetrahedrons using a range of materials. Who can make the strongest, weakest or most flexible tetrahedron? How can you make the tests fair using different materials?

NC mathematics objectives

- Identify 3-D shapes (Year 5 geometry – properties of shapes);
- Recognise, describe and build simple 3-D shapes (Year 6 geometry – properties of shapes).

NC science objectives

- Compare and group together everyday materials on the basis of their properties, including their hardness, solubility, transparency, conductivity and response to magnets (Year 5 properties and changes of materials);
- Give reasons, based on evidence from comparative and fair tests, for the particular uses of everyday materials, including metals, wood and plastic (Year 5 properties and changes of materials).

Teaching tip

Position the tetrahedron over a gap between two tables. This way, if the tetrahedron collapses, it can crash land on the floor and not someone's hand or table!

Figure 7.8 Skeletal tetrahedron with 6.1 kg attached and still holding!

Topic: Gold

Mathematics-led activity: The painted cube

This is a well-known mathematics activity. Ask learners to imagine a 3 × 3 × 3 cube, which has been painted gold all over! The task is to work out how many of the individual cubes have 1, 2 or 3 faces with gold on them. Ask learners initially to make the large cube out of multilink (Figure 7.9). This will help them to visualise how the smaller cubes fit together to make the larger one. It will also help them to work out how many smaller cubes have faces painted with gold. This activity helps learners to visualise the properties of a cube and also encourages them to use correct mathematical language and reasoning such as faces and vertices.

Clue: there will only be one cube that will not have any gold on it!

This activity can be extended to think about a 4 × 4 × 4 cube or an even bigger one! Encourage learners to work mathematically using their knowledge and understanding of fluency, reasoning and problem solving (see Chapter 2). An extra challenge is to ask them to draw a representation of the larger cube on paper. Isometric paper will be useful here.

NC mathematics objectives

- Draw 2-D shapes and make 3-D shapes using modelling materials; recognise 3-D shapes in different orientations and describe them (Year 3 geometry – properties of shapes);

- Identify 3-D shapes, including cubes and other cuboids, from 2-D representations (Year 5 geometry – properties of shapes).

Science-led activity: Is gold a rock?

Linking on from the painted cube, ask the learners if they think gold is a rock. Can they explain their reasons? Can they explain what a rock is?

Tell learners they are going to become rock detectives. Go for a walk around school. Ask them to write down or draw any examples of objects or materials they think are made from rock (e.g. playground, bricks, tiles, benches). Ask learners to try and describe the rocks, using words such as strong, rigid, rough, shiny, dull, waterproof.

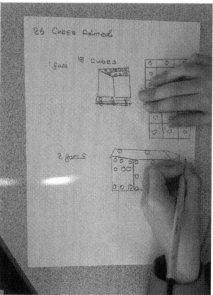

Figure 7.9 Learners solve the cube problem

The following website may be of help: www.bbc.co.uk/bitesize/ks2/science/materials/rocks_soils/play/.

Using a collection of rocks, investigate different properties found in each one (e.g. do they have grains, crystals or fossils in them?). Discover where different rocks come from and how fossils are formed. What happens when rocks are rubbed together or placed in water?

NC science objectives

- Record findings using simple scientific language, drawings, labelled diagrams, keys, bar charts and tables (Lower Key Stage 1 working scientifically);

- Compare and group together different kinds of rocks on the basis of their appearance and simple physical properties (Year 3 rocks);

- Describe in simple terms how fossils are formed when things that have lived are trapped within rock (Year 3 rocks).

Teaching tip

Gold is not a rock, it is an element, a metal found in rock. Metals that are found in rocks are called ores. For more information, refer to Chapter 14: Materials.

Conclusion

This chapter has explored how the two areas within geometry (position and direction, and properties of shape) are connected to science in different ways. It has shown that we live in a geometric world and that we often use this knowledge in a non-mathematical way. Much of geometry in school is about sorting and classifying, thinking up and testing conjectures and making sense of experiences, all of which are the skills we employ when working scientifically.

Summary of learning

In this chapter, you will have learned:

- the key points in teaching geometry;
- how geometry and science have worked together to help shape some of the most beautiful and ground-breaking buildings we have today;
- that geometry in mathematics can often have a different understanding from that in everyday life.

8

Statistics

This chapter will ensure that you:

- have a good understanding of statistics and data handling as part of science and mathematics;

- understand how data handling positively affects aspects of learners' understanding of mathematics and science.

Overview

Statistics (also known as data handling) is a branch of mathematics that deals with the presentation and use of data. It involves the collection, organisation, representation and interpretation of data to answer a question, to deal with a problem or as part of an investigation. The mathematics curriculum (DfE, 2013) includes objectives for statistics from Year 2 to Year 6, while the science programmes of study draw heavily on this area within working scientifically.

An example of a mathematician

Alan Mathison Turing is famous for his work as a code breaker at Bletchley Park during the Second World War. He was a mathematician, a computer scientist and a cryptanalyst or code breaker (Figure 8.1). He and his team – in the now famous 'hut eight' – devised a number of techniques for breaking German ciphers (algorithms for performing encryption of messages). His understanding and use of data and statistics in code breaking meant that the Allies could read secret German communications. This work is celebrated across Europe and the wider world, as it shortened the Second World War and perhaps saved many thousands of lives.

Figure 8.1 Pencil sketch of Alan Turing (1912–1954)

Connecting mathematics and science: statistics

An important part of mathematics and science is quantifying phenomena so that they can be better described, predicted and considered. Much of what we see in the world initially looks chaotic, such as the weather and animal behaviour. We look to science and mathematics to find order in what often appears an unpredictable world. Statistics allow mathematicians and scientists to look at phenomena such as the tides, the weather and the movement of the planets to gather information, usually large sets of data, which allow us to describe the phenomena precisely. Patterns are often discernible within sets of data; for example, there are higher wind speeds in certain months of the year or when atmospheric pressure is low. The identification of pattern in data or statistics is very powerful, as it allows more accurate predictions, for example, by extrapolating not yet tested values.

A real-life example with mathematics and science

We see data used in many ways every day. You may recall the story of these dramatic events from August 1970 when Jim Lovell calmly reported from space, '*Houston, we have a problem*'. His words were heard by a Houston mission control room buzzing with data and statistics. What followed was a fantastic example of teams working together on complex problem solving: one team worked

Figure 8.2 Launch of Apollo 13

on how the astronauts could fashion a cartridge to collect CO_2 from the air to avoid suffocation, while other teams looked at data about the health and well being of the astronauts, data about the fuel and temperature of the spacecraft, data on the flight path of the capsule and no doubt much more. Decisions had to be made and problems solved based on masses of numerical data. Getting the use of energy wrong, running out of air or plotting the wrong flight path would have resulted in the deaths of the astronauts. For those who have read Lovell and Kluger's (1994) book or seen the film *Apollo 13* (directed by Ron Howard), the safe return of the astronauts seemed like a miracle, whereas in fact the mission was saved by problem solving informed by mathematics and science (Figure 8.2).

Key teaching points for statistics

Essentially, there are four stages to handling data and statistics (collecting, organising, representing and interpreting). that learners should experience throughout their science and mathematics learning. Within each stage there are a number of different activities and approaches that can be used to draw on skills within working mathematically and scientifically. One example would be collecting data by designing questionnaires or conducting surveys. Similarly, when learners are ready to organise and represent the data, careful choices need to be made about the best type of graph or chart to use. Often, the way data is represented can influence the way it is interpreted.

Graphs, charts, tables and diagrams can be used to represent both mathematical and scientific data. As Deboys and Pitt (1988) noted, *'One picture is worth a thousand words'*. While there are many different ways to represent data, we have selected the ones that are used most often in primary classrooms across mathematics and science:

- Tally chart – a technique used to collect data, based on counting in fives;
- Frequency table – a graphical means of showing the amount of data collected in each group;
- Bar chart – a frequency diagram using rectangles of equal width whose heights or lengths are proportional to the frequency;
- Venn diagram – a way of organising data pictorially, showing the relationship between sets and subsets of data;
- Block graph – a bar chart where the bars themselves are divided to mark off each individual piece of data;
- Pictogram – a frequency diagram using a symbol to represent units of data;
- Pie chart – a circular frequency diagram using sectors at angles to the centre. Often these sectors or proportions are written as percentages. Pie charts are really only appropriate for discrete data with a small number of subsets;
- Carroll diagram – sometimes called a two-way table, a diagram used for grouping items in a yes/no fashion;
- Line graph – used to represent statistical data and should only really be used where the horizontal axis is 'time';
- Scatter diagram – also called a scatter plot, scattergram or scattergraph, shows how two sets of numerical data are related, by considering matching pairs of numbers as coordinates and then plotting them as a single point.

Another important distinction within this mathematical and scientific area is between discrete and continuous data (see also Chapter 9). Discrete means separate, and so it follows that discrete data relate to categories that are separate from one another. For example, how learners travel to school would use discrete data (e.g. on foot, by bike, by car, on a bus). Continuous data are quite different; they are connected, usually because they are numeric. An example of continuous data would be the height of a sunflower plant over a period of time. The National Curriculum (DfE, 2013) for science requires the use of dataloggers, which is a great way to collect data sets of continuous data and so develop statistical skills (see Chapter 9 for examples of using dataloggers).

> ### Teaching tip
> When teaching learners to use tables and graphs in mathematics and science, try to avoid doing all the preparation for them. They will learn more by constructing the tables and graphs themselves.

Teaching activities linking mathematics to science

Key Stage 1

Topic: Pond dipping

(If your school doesn't have a pond, you could set up a small barrel or cut down a water butt seeded with water and weed from an existing garden pond. You might even do similar work based on a pile of leaves, sticks or logs.)

Pond dipping is a great activity to engage learners in, especially because it encourages learning outside the classroom. Remind learners to have their containers half full before they start! 'Pond detectives' usually sweep their nets in a figure-of-eight motion (this is thought to catch more pond life than just sweeping back and forth). Empty the contents of the net into the container and investigate.

You might talk to learners about the number of times they sweep the nets. For example, if some learners are sweeping theirs ten times and others are sweeping only once, is this fair? This also ensures they are working scientifically. Ask learners to count how many creatures they have in their containers. The use of a spoon and a hand lens helps for closer inspections. Ask learners to record their data using tally charts, bar charts or a pictogram, thus enabling them to represent all the different creatures they find (Figure 8.3). As you are outside, why not record the data next to the pond and take a photograph as evidence?

To extend the activity, you could investigate how healthy your pond is by assigning it a biotic index, which is a scale that shows the quality of an environment by indicating the types of organisms that are present in it. Each organism is given a value, which contributes to an overall total. Learners could work out which animal has the highest score in their container. Is this the same for all of the containers? Is the pond of good quality? What reasons can they offer? Can they use their observations to help answer these questions?

You can find a biotic index for fresh water at the following websites:

http://www.nationalinsectweek.co.uk/pond_dipping/is_your_stream_healthy.htm

http://watermonitoring.uwex.edu/wav/monitoring/biotic.html

Pond dipping can be carried out over a short amount of time or over a longer period, allowing results to be compared. Learners could explore how the animals in the pond habitat change throughout the year. They could consider how to group the different animals, perhaps using a biotic index, or they could make their own simple key. They could also consider the human impact (positive and negative) on the pond environment.

So far, this activity has used many more mathematical skills than just those associated with statistics, including ones we would associate with working mathematically (fluency, reasoning and problem solving). However, the objectives below link pond dipping to objectives within statistics, as well as some of the science objectives covered through this context too.

NC mathematics objectives

• Interpret and construct simple pictograms, tally charts, block diagrams and simple tables (Year 2 statistics);

• Ask and answer simple questions by counting the number of objects in each category and sorting the categories by quantity (Year 2 statistics).

NC science objectives

• Perform simple tests (Key Stage 1 working scientifically);

• Identify and classify (Key Stage 1 working scientifically);

• Identify and name a variety of common animals that are carnivores, herbivores and omnivores (Year 1 animals, including humans).

Teaching tip
Smaller learners can always kneel at the edge of the pond, helping them avoid toppling in!

Figure 8.3 A bar chart to show the number of creatures from a sample dip

Topic: Handa's Surprise

Using a fiction book provides a fantastic activity to base learning on. Handa's Surprise (Browne, 2006) is a story about a girl who takes a basket of fruit to her friend Akeyo. On her way, Handa wonders which of the fruits her friend will like the best. However, as she walks, carrying the basket of fruit on her head, various animals steal the fruit, so that when she finds her friend and gives her the basket of fruit, it is Handa who has the biggest surprise of all!

Mathematics-led activity: Favourite fruit

Explore which are the learners' favourite fruit or which fruit learners currently have in their fridge, and represent this either as a 'fruit' block chart or as a numerical block chart (Figure 8.4). Learners could also discover which type of fruit has travelled the furthest and show this in order from the nearest to the furthest.

NC mathematics objectives

- Interpret and construct simple pictograms, tally charts, block diagrams and simple tables (Year 2 statistics);

- Ask and answer questions about totalling and comparing categorical data (Year 2 statistics).

Science-led activity: Nutrition

Learners could discuss the importance of exercise and nutrition for humans. They could consider why Handa was taking a basket of fruit to her friend and why this was important. Or, they could discuss what other types of food could have been in the basket and whether these would be considered important in helping us to keep healthy.

NC science objectives

- Describe the importance for humans of exercise, eating the right amounts of different types of food, and hygiene (Year 2 animals, including humans);

- Find out about and describe the basic needs of animals, including humans, for survival (water, food and air) (Year 2 animals, including humans).

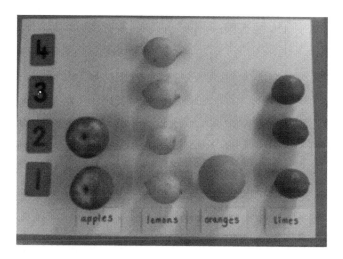

Figure 8.4 Chart showing favourite types of fruit

Key Stage 2

Topic: Code detectives

Most learners love solving puzzles and problems, so this activity uses both their mathematical and scientific skills to do just that. We have already mentioned the important work that Alan Turing and his colleagues did to help hasten the end to the Second World War with his famous code breaking Enigma machine. This activity challenges learners to make their own Enigma machine using two sheets of A4 paper, a tube (75 mm in diameter and at least 225 mm long), some Sellotape© and a pair of scissors. This activity is a variation of function machines that mathematics activities often use to solve number problems.

You can download the printable pages at: http://wiki.franklinheath. co.uk/index.php/Enigma/Paper_Enigma. Alternatively, the following website provides a template to make your own Enigma machine. Follow the instructions and you should end up with an Enigma machine that looks like the one we made and shown in Figure 8.5.

Once learners have their own machine make sure that the grey bars on the reflector and the input/output cylinders line up, as this is the start of the machine and lets you track the positions of the other cylinders as they move around. Now they can start sending codes to each other. To begin, challenge them just to write short words of a few letters each. This activity focuses on the importance of data, a skill that runs through the heart of both science and mathematics. It also links strongly with computational theory in computing.

NC mathematics objectives

- Interpret and present data (Year 3 statistics);
- Complete, read and interpret information (Year 5 statistics).

NC science objectives

- Gather, record, classify and present data (Lower Key Stage 2 working scientifically);
- Record data and results (Upper Key Stage 2 working scientifically).

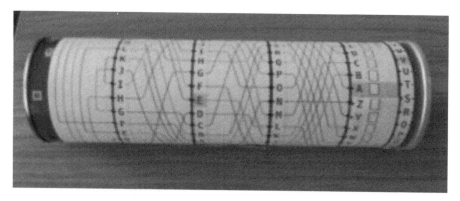

Figure 8.5 Homemade Enigma machine

Topic: Chocolate

Mathematics-led activity: Do all boxes of Smarties© contain the same numbers of each colour?

This activity works particularly well if each pair or group of learners has its own box of Smarties© to investigate. However, coloured counters can be used as a substitute!

Set learners the question 'Do all boxes of Smarties© contain the same number and colour?' Explain that you would like to see the data presented in at least three different ways so that the class can consider which is the most effective and ineffective representation of data for this investigation. A reminder of the different types of graphs and charts may be useful here (a list of the most frequently used graphs and charts is included in the first half of this chapter). Use this opportunity to discuss the difference between discrete and continuous data. Establish that this data set is discrete, so this eliminates the use of line graphs, for example.

Learners will probably start by tipping out their Smarties© and sorting them into their different colours (Figure 8.6). Once learners have presented their data in at least three different ways, discuss the advantages and disadvantages of each one? Return to the original question: what is the answer?

This activity can be extended to investigate other questions. Here are a few suggestions:

1. Which is the most popular colour of Smarties© in your pack? In all the packs?

2. Find the mode, median and mean of the number of Smarties© in each pack.

3. Choose two colours and compare data from 10 different packs (for example, blue and red Smarties©).

4. Work out the percentage of brown Smarties© in the pack.

5. What is the ratio of green Smarties© to orange Smarties©?

6. What is the probability of finding a green Smartie© in your tube?

NC mathematics objectives

- Interpret and present data using bar charts, pictograms and tables (Year 3 statistics);

- Interpret and present discrete and continuous data using appropriate graphical methods, including bar charts and time graphs (Year 4 statistics);

- Interpret and present discrete and continuous data using appropriate graphical methods, including bar charts and time graphs (Year 5 statistics);

- Interpret and construct pie charts and line graphs and use these to solve problems (Year 6 statistics).

Science-led activity: Is chocolate good for us?

If learners have just completed the above investigation using Smarties©, it is likely they are going to want to eat them! So, this provides the perfect link to exploring which foods are healthy/unhealthy and which foods our bodies need to gain the right amount of nutrients to keep us in good health.

Start by asking learners to make a list or draw foods that they think are healthy and those that are not. Do they think chocolate is good for us? Explain there are many different viewpoints regarding this question. For example, some scientists have found that chocolate may help older people keep their brains healthy and their thinking sharp (www.livescience.com).

Explain that our bodies need a balanced diet to work properly. (For more information, see Chapter 15: Animal Biology). This means eating the right amount of food from the four main food groups and drinking plenty of water. Ask learners to sort a range of items into the four different food groups: carbohydrates, proteins, fats and vitamins. Use either pictures or real objects for learners to sort. Ask how they will display the data? This also reminds learners to use their data handling skills, which they used previously in the Smarties© investigation.

Include items such as bread, potatoes, pasta, fish, eggs, cheese, meat, nuts, butter, chips, chocolate, fruits, vegetables and milk. Learners often think that fat is not good for us. However, we need all of the food groups to maintain healthy bodies, so as long as we eat in moderation, a little chocolate each week is okay as a treat!

To extend this activity, learners could design some posters with top tips on how to eat healthily, using the four main food groups and their data handling skills to display the information.

NC science objectives

- Identify that animals, including humans, need a nutritious diet, and that they cannot make their own food; they get nutrition from what they eat (Year 3 animals, including humans);

- Recognise the impact of diet, exercise, drugs and lifestyle on the way bodies function (Year 6 animals, including humans).

Teaching tip

Often we only focus on one type of graph or chart (e.g. a pie chart). However, this limits learners' understanding as to why we use different types of representations for different data sets. To extend and master this mathematical and scientific area, it is often more effective to present one set of data in a variety of ways and then, for example, to consider which is the clearest, the most helpful or the most biased.

 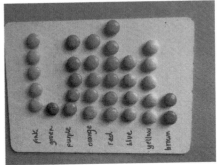

Figure 8.6 Smarties© grouped by colour and using a bar chart

Conclusion

This chapter has explored an area of mathematics and science that is connected in a particularly strong way. When we use data, it is often hard to know if we are using mathematical or scientific skills. The very nature of using data in mathematics assumes a context, which can often lend itself perfectly to working scientifically.

Summary of learning

In this chapter, you will have learned:

- the four stages involved in statistics;
- some of the different ways data can be organised and represented;
- that data can be discrete or continuous;
- that science and mathematics integrate powerfully in the area of statistics/data handling;
- about a range of examples where learners can learn mathematics and science in meaningful ways.

9

Working Scientifically

This chapter will ensure that you:

- have a well-developed understanding of how mathematics contributes to working scientifically;

- understand how science enquiry benefits from mathematics;

- can identify opportunities to use working scientifically in science to enrich and strengthen meaningful learning in both subjects.

Overview

Working scientifically, an important part of the National Curriculum (DfE, 2013), includes the skills and knowledge of science enquiry and the encouragement of curiosity. Working scientifically involves different types of scientific enquiry: observing over time; pattern seeking; identifying, classifying and grouping; comparative and fair testing (controlled investigations); and researching using secondary sources (Turner, 2012).

Primary teachers are encouraged to teach science and mathematics through practical activities and investigation (DfE, 2013; Ofsted, 2013). The link between achievement in science and classroom practical work has been challenged (Hodson, 1993; Hofstein and Lunetta, 2004), although much reported research was conducted with older pupils. What is clear is that we should not assume that practical work alone is enough to teach science. It would appear that the structure, scaffolding and challenge provided by skilled teachers are key to ensuring that the potential of practical investigation is realised. Ofsted reports on science have repeatedly advocated learner engagement in science enquiry and the development of science skills (Ofsted, 2011, 2013). Science can be counter-intuitive and at times challenging. When learners use science in simple or other more developed investigations, more of them can make sense of the science.

Figure 9.1 Photograph of Gregor Mendel (1822–1884)

An example of a scientist

When looking at a beautiful bouquet of flowers, do you see science at work? The flowers and plants can be studied and classified but what about the plant breeding that helped produce the amazing blooms? For many hundreds of years, farmers and plant breeders have selected plants with particular characteristics knowing that a proportion of the offspring will have the same desirable characteristics, such as a particular colour, a larger edible root or fruit, or resistance to disease. Plant breeding is now a branch of science in its own right, but with the advent of genetically modified plants it has become more contentious. The father of this science of genetics was Gregor Mendel (1822–1884), an Austrian monk whose work was not celebrated until years after his death (Figure 9.1). He kept careful records of his plant breeding with peas. He realised that when he bred two plants of the same species with different characteristics, there were patterns in the numbers of young displaying each characteristic. This is the mathematical world of probability, where Mendel found the likely characteristics of offspring were by no means random.

His was a science that relied on mathematics, proportions, statistics and on working scientifically. He planned and carried out tests, predicted, measured, counted, observed and recorded what he saw. He discovered that different pairings of parents produce different ratios of young displaying parental characteristics. This is because some traits or characteristics are more dominant than others in their inheritance and this affects the proportions of young displaying a particular characteristic.

Mendel did not live to see the discovery of DNA, the biological mechanism that controls what he observed. His own discoveries, however, were very valuable and led to the science of genetics. (See Chapter 5 on pattern for a DNA activity.)

Find more about genetics at http://www.dnaftb.org/1/. Find out more about Mendel at http://www.biography.com/people/gregor-mendel-39282.

Connecting mathematics and science: working scientifically

By combining mathematics and science, the two subjects are enriched and learners of both subjects enabled. The power of mathematics as a language of relationships and values is employed in meaningful science contexts. Science, and in particular working scientifically, shows learners that the real world is a place to explore but where values and relationships allow us to be systematic in our investigations.

In the English mathematics curriculum (DfE, 2013), teachers are tasked to work mathematically by the three overall aims of fluency, reasoning and problem solving. As we saw in Chapter 2 science, and in particular working scientifically, provides a context for learners to develop mathematical fluency in the context of investigations and problem-solving scenarios. Reasoning arises in all aspects of science as we seek to explain what we observe and link the science to the real world. For example, if all the plants I observe are green, I might reason that all plants are green.

The human condition experiment

One school used psychology as a basis for science, employing statistics to challenge learners in a topic entitled 'The Human Condition'. After a series of preparation tasks and games, the class generated ideas for potential experiments to reveal influences on human preferences. Groups of learners proposed several ideas, which they then presented to a panel of teachers who selected a study to go forward to the experimental stage.

The learners planned the testing including the experimental procedure (Figure 9.2). They ensured that no clues were left in the room and that the recording slips were designed and suitable for the planned tests. In this example, the group of three learners wanted to test whether in a taste test of different brands of cola, children would be influenced by the brand (Figure 9.3). This was their theory.

Test 1: This was the control group. Children were asked to rate three anonymous cola drinks.

Test 2: These children were told that they were doing a test to see if people prefer branded colas. The colas were served from anonymous bottles but with the appropriate bottle tops in place as a clue.

Test 3: These children were shown different bottles and told that the three samples represented three different brands of cola.

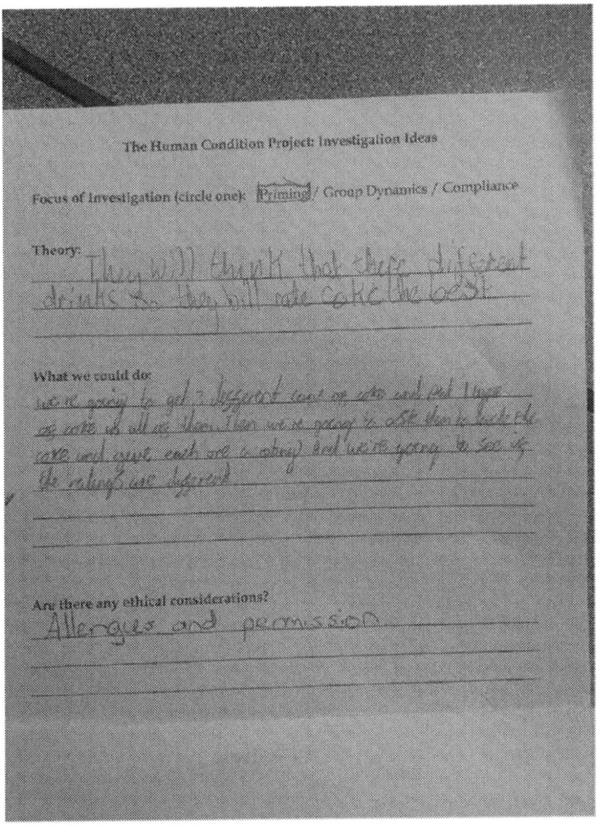

The Human Condition Project: Investigation Ideas

Focus of Investigation (circle one): Priming / Group Dynamics / Compliance

Theory: They will think that there different drinks & they will rate coke the best

What we could do: we're going to get 3 different cans of coke and put three of coke in all of them. Then we're going to ask them to taste the coke and give each one a rating and we're going to see if the ratings are different

Are there any ethical considerations? Allergues and permssion

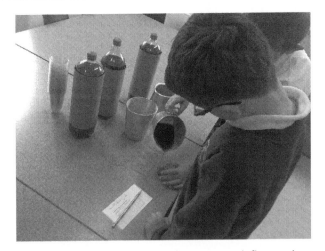

Figure 9.2 Plan for the human condition experiment

Figure 9.3 Year 6 testing how children's preferences are influenced

Table 9.1 Results of the cola taste tests

	Group 1: Control group, no product information			Group 2: Bottle labels covered but Coca Cola logo visible on the lid of B			Group 3: Children were told that each sample was a brand of cola as below		
	All ratings out of ten			All ratings out of ten			All ratings out of ten		
	A	B	C	A	B	C	A	B	C
							Tesco value brand	Coca Cola	Tesco Classic
	8	5	10	8	7	10	8	8	9
	7	5	4	8	9	8	5	9	10
	10	8	6	9	10	9	9	10	7
	8	9	10	7	8	5	8	9	7
	6	8	9	7	5	8	9	6	7
	5	3	9	8	7	6	9	10	4
	7	5	6	5	7	5	9	4	10
	7	6	7	9	6	10	8	9	10
	9	10	7	5	8	8			
Totals	67	59	68	66	67	69	65	65	64
Mean	7.4	6.5	7.5	7.2	7.3	7.6	8.1	8.1	8.0

Table 9.1 shows their results. These data led the class to consider whether the results disproved their proposed theory, and whether such factors as experimental error had influenced the results. For instance, were some cola samples going flat during the experiment and affecting the results? Their teacher also raised the question of sample size. Having designed and carried out the experiment, the learners were in a strong position to evaluate the results.

Questions lead to investigations

It is clear that both mathematics and science utilise questions, such as: What is the largest prime number? Are all metals magnetic? A question that can be answered scientifically is the starting point for pupils working scientifically. These questions can come from teachers but increasingly in the primary years, learners should be given the opportunity to answer questions they have posed themselves. Taking time at the start of a topic to elicit what learners already know will often reveal aspects they want to find out about. The following are some questions that might lead to science enquiries:

- Can we see evidence for global warming in our weather?
- As a pendulum string gets longer, what happens to the number of swings per minute?
- What is the ideal wind speed for drying wet fabric?
- Which material makes the 'grippiest' soles for shoes?
- Do woodlice prefer damp, dry, light or dark conditions?

Teaching tip

Teachers often help learners structure their thoughts about working scientifically with various writing or thinking frames, such as that shown in Table 9.2.

As learners become familiar with working scientifically, they can begin to provide a rationale for their choice of enquiry (see Table 9.2). They might be asked to consider a question and select the appropriate form of enquiry. In the right-hand column of Table 9.2, learners can explain how they might use that form of enquiry before making a choice.

Working mathematically involves thinking about the question posed, what the likely answer might be and how it might be solved. In a similar way, working scientifically uses a question to consider a prediction and then a plan for an investigation to answer the question. Learners' questions in science and mathematics are often naïve, so you will need to model or assist the learners in rephrasing their questions. This iteration of the question can occur more than once and mirrors common practice in real science contexts, as in the lesson on thermal insulation below.

Table 9.2 Which type of enquiry might learners employ?

Our question is ...	What type of enquiry will I use?
Observation over time?	
Identifying, grouping and classifying?	
Pattern seeking?	
Research using secondary resources?	
Fair testing?	
Observation over time?	

In a lesson on thermal insulation, one class suggested the following question:

'Which material is best?'

Their teacher asked them to explain the word 'best' and to rephrase the question, which became:

'Which material keeps the ice lolly cold?'

The teacher checked that they understood the words 'material' and 'cold'. Later, they rephrased the question as:

'Which material keeps the ice lolly colder for longer?'

Each iteration improves the question – that is, makes it more scientific. The final question requires measurement of temperature and time, so that mathematics assists the learners in their investigation. The learners could quantify the relationship between two variables (temperature and time).

Both mathematics and science are about relationships – these can be spatial, algebraic or proportional. For example, in working scientifically we often consider the relationship of cause and effect: if we vary one thing, what will happen to another? For example, how much we stretch an elastic band will affect the distance the toy car attached to it is propelled. The systematic changes made to variables in science tests allow a pattern to be identified, or not. For example, raising the temperature of a solvent (water) results in the solute (jelly) being dissolved more quickly. In order to vary these values systematically and establish usable patterns, we need to quantify the variables. Younger primary learners will not always use numbers but will use qualitative descriptors and categoric data, e.g. temperature will be 'cold, warm and hot', force will be 'tiny, small, medium and large'. With measurement, however, we move from qualitative judgements to quantitative measures (Table 9.3).

Thus measurement is an important aspect of working scientifically and of working mathematically. Science enables meaningful measurement in the context of an investigation, the opportunity to develop skills. Mathematics allows the use of number in measures to be systematic and to quantify values and changes we make or observe.

Science also allows the use of a wider range of measures than in most mathematics lessons. Chapter 6 (Measurement) refers to the internationally agreed measures known as SI units, used by mathematicians and scientists throughout the world. Measuring requires measuring equipment, which we illustrate throughout this book (Chapter 13, for example, illustrates a light meter and a decibel meter). Data loggers offer the opportunity to gather data on light, sound, temperature, pulse rate and more. They can operate away from the computer and will also download data to your computer quickly. Figure 9.4 shows how a class recorded data over twenty-four hours. Not surprisingly, the temperature did not fluctuate greatly. Can you see which fluctuated most, light or

Table 9.3 Qualitative and qualitative measures (units listed here are all SI units)

Phenomena	Can be described qualitatively	Is measured in ... units	Using a device called a ...	These devices come in different forms
Level of heat	With the sense of touch and the language of hot, hotter, cold and colder	Degrees centigrade (°C)	Thermometer	Digital and analogue, maximum and minimum, data logger
Sound	With the sense of hearing and the language of loud, louder, quiet, quieter, silent	Decibels (dB)	Decibel meter	Analogue, digital including data logger
Light	With the sense of sight and the language of dark, light, lighter, bright, brighter	Lux (lx)	Light metre	Analogue, digital including data logger
Force	With the sense of touch, the pressure applied and the language of push, pull, bigger	Newton (N)	Newton metre	Analogue, digital including data logger
Distance	With non-standard measures, e.g. carpet tiles, strides, hand spans, lengths of string, etc.	Millimetres (mm), centimetres (cm), metres (m), kilometres (km)	Rulers, tape measures, etc.	Analogue, digital
Time	By estimating and counting, e.g. 1 elephant, 2 elephants, 3 elephants for 3 seconds	Seconds, minutes, hours, days, weeks, months, years	Clocks, sand timers, ticker timers, water clocks, etc.	Analogue, digital
Capacity	By comparison, this container holds more/less, largest, smallest, etc.	Millilitres (mL), litres (L)	Measuring cylinder, jug or syringe	Analogue

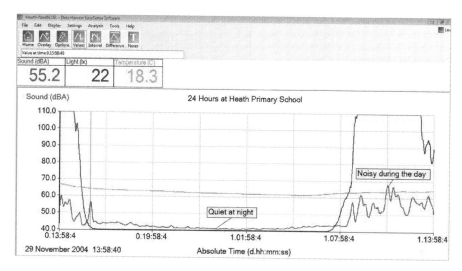

Figure 9.4 Data gathered in real time overnight in a classroom (Reproduced with permission from Data Harvest Group (http://www.data-harvest.co.uk/catalogue/science/primary/datalogging))

noise? Can you reason and explain these changes? Are you doing mathematics or science?

Some data collected by learners will be categoric (discrete) in nature, such as type of pet, hair colour and day of the week (Figure 9.5). These are categoric because there is a value we call Tuesday and another we call Wednesday, for example, but nothing in between (say, Tuesdaywednesday!). Continuous data, in contrast, are measured on a continuous scale with numerous subdivisions. For example, time is measured in days, which can be subdivided into hours, which

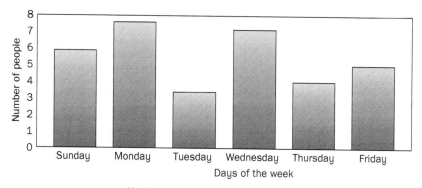

Number of Birthdays on Days of the Week

Figure 9.5 Categoric data: graph showing birthdays

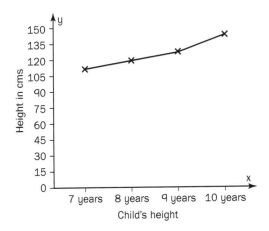

Figure 9.6 Continuous data: height of a child in centimetres over four years

are themselves divisible into minutes, and so on. Figure 9.6 illustrates continuous data where values (time and height) can be divided and subdivided. Table 9.4 provides examples of different data types. (For more on discrete and continuous data, see Chapter 8: Statistics.)

A real-life example with mathematics and science

The food industry makes extensive use of mathematics and the scientific method in trialling and testing the safety and quality of food. You will hear, occasionally, of food scares, which reinforce our need to understand food and what we eat. At almost every stage of food production, dates are recorded and values such as temperature measured. Food packaging includes a great deal of information, some of which is presented as words, some graphically and much as numbers, including mass, date of manufacture, sell-by date, consume-by date, calorific value, the percentage of (or grams of) fat, carbohydrates, sugar and salt, and proportions of daily recommended values.

Table 9.4 Examples of different data types

Continuous data	Categoric data
age	hair colour, eye colour
body measures, e.g. hand span, height, mass	types of animal
temperature	eye colour
sound	days
length	months

Key teaching points for working scientifically

Working scientifically is the most enjoyable part of science for many learners and for a teacher to teach. It is the point in science when learners can pose questions and look for answers themselves. It allows mathematics and language to be used in very meaningful contexts. Working scientifically can be taught by modelling the skills and the process of enquiry, such as the accurate measurement of temperature of a cooling liquid over time or the classification of materials that might be suitable for soundproofing. The teaching of working scientifically can be challenging, as it is usually taught over a series of lessons, requires equipment and often (though not always) requires learners to work together in pairs or groups. When conducting a test in biology (e.g. growth tests with plants), it may extend over several days, so you will need lesson time to plan and set up the test, time to make measurements each day, and time to make use of the data and form some conclusions.

Teaching tip

Make sure you plan opportunities to teach mathematics and science skills, particularly if equipment is involved, e.g. arranging a plain light background and good light when using a magnifier and selecting the scale on a graph to best represent the statistics.

Teaching activities linking mathematics to science

Key Stage 1

Topic: Clothing

Activity: Clothing for Tigger

'Materials' is a very useful aspect of science for working scientifically. Learners can investigate:

- how waterproof fabrics are;
- how strong fabrics are;
- how reflective the colours of fabrics are;
- which fabrics people like;
- whether materials are opaque or transparent.

Explain that a character known to the learners – in this instance Tigger the tiger – requires warm clothing for the winter, for a holiday or an adventure. After asking learners to suggest materials, challenge them to examine a set of materials and to predict which would make good thermal insulators. Explore how many different combinations Tigger could wear. Ask the learners to devise a test to compare the thermal properties of different materials. They might consider, for example, which material will keep a water bottle warm for longest?

NC science objectives

- Ask simple questions and recognise that they can be answered in different ways (Key Stage 1 working scientifically);
- Observe closely, using simple equipment (Key Stage 1 working scientifically);
- Perform simple tests (Key Stage 1 working scientifically);
- Identify and classify (Key Stage 1 working scientifically);
- Use observations and ideas to suggest answers to questions (Key Stage 1 working scientifically);
- Gather and record data to help in answering questions (Key Stage 1 working scientifically);
- Describe the simple physical properties of a variety of everyday materials (Year 1 everyday materials);
- Compare and group together a variety of everyday materials on the basis of their simple physical properties (Year 1 everyday materials).

NC mathematics objectives

- Choose and use appropriate standard units to estimate and measure, for example, temperature (°C) to the nearest appropriate unit using thermometers (Year 2 measurement);

Topic: Conditions for healthy plant growth

Activity: What is the effect of light on plant growth?

Introduce learners to a poster of Confused Colin (Figure 9.7). Colin claims that plants don't need light to grow. Ask learners to talk about plants and their need for light. Do they agree with Colin? Can they devise a test to prove to Colin that they are right?

- Solve problems with addition and subtraction (Year 2 number – addition and subtraction;

- Ask and answer questions about totalling and comparing categoric data (Year 2 statistics);

- Interpret and construct simple pictograms, tally charts, block diagrams and simple tables (Year 2 statistics).

Encourage learners to devise their own comparative test. Ask them to describe what they plan to do and explain why they have chosen their method. Ask them to plan the test(s) detailing their question, prediction, method, equipment, what they will record, how often, in which units of measurement and how they will record the data.

One option would be to grow some seedlings in light and some in the dark. The height of the seedlings could be measured each day for a week.

NC science objectives

- Ask simple questions and recognise that they can be answered in different ways (Key Stage 1 working scientifically);

- Observe closely, using simple equipment (Key Stage 1 working scientifically);

- Perform simple tests (Key Stage 1 working scientifically);

- Identify and classify (Key Stage 1 working scientifically);

- Use observations and ideas to suggest answers to questions (Key Stage 1 working scientifically);

- Gather and record data to help in answering questions (Key Stage 1 working scientifically).

- Observe and describe how seeds and bulbs grow into mature plants (Year 2 plants);

- Find out and describe how plants need water, light and a suitable temperature to grow and stay healthy (Year 2 plants).

NC mathematics objectives

- Compare, describe and solve practical problems for lengths and heights (Year 1 measurement);

- Ask and answer questions about totalling and comparing categoric data (Year 2 statistics).

Figure 9.7 Format for letter to Confused Colin

Key Stage 2

Topic: Rocks in our locality

Activity: Classifying our set of rocks

Rocks can be tested for hardness by designing scratch tests or for permeability by immersing them in 100 ml of water for 10 minutes to see if water is absorbed. They can also be used to teach the skills of identification, grouping and classifying. Colour illustrations are very useful, as are hand lenses for identification of rocks. Learners can also use a simple key to identify rocks (see Figure 9.8). In order to teach the skill of classification, give learners a partly constructed key and ask them to add another rock. You could also utilise published field guides or keys.

You could give learners a collection of rocks and tell them astronauts found them on a mystery planet. Their job is to describe, name and classify these rocks for other scientists. You might later reveal the mystery planet is Earth. Rocks you might use for these lessons could include: granite, slate, chalk, limestone, sandstone, marble and quartz. Such information can be presented in a number of ways (see Table 9.5 for an example).

The following are some useful websites:

See http://www.crickweb.co.uk/ks1science.html#groupinganimals for a KS1 sorting game

See http://www.teachingandlearningresources.co.uk/key.shtml for a KS2 branching key game

See http://primary.naace.co.uk/activities/sorting_games/ for a useful set of sorting games

See http://interactivesites.weebly.com/rocks-and-minerals.html for recognising rocks

NC science objectives

- Compare and group together different kinds of rocks on the basis of their appearance and simple physical properties (Year 3 rocks);
- Gather, record, classify and present data in a variety of ways to help in answering questions (Lower Key Stage 2 working scientifically).

NC mathematics objectives

- Measure, compare, add and subtract lengths (m, cm, mm) (Year 3 measurement);
- Interpret and present data using bar charts, pictograms and tables (Year 3 statistics).

Table 9.5 Carroll diagram – rocks

	Dark coloured rocks	*Light coloured rocks*
Crystals visible	granite	
Crystals not visible	slate	chalk, limestone, marble

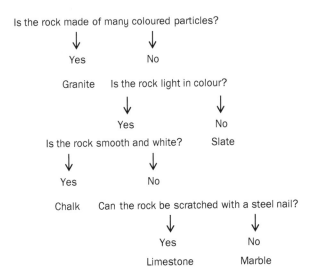

Figure 9.8 Branching key for rocks

Topic: Keeping warm

Activity: Pingu's thermals

Ask learners how they keep warm in cold weather. Focus on clothing, layers of clothing and types of suitable materials. Introduce a context such as artic explorers or Pingu the Penguin and explain that they need to keep warm in very cold conditions. Discuss what the temperature would be, thus linking to negative numbers. Ask them to design, predict the outcome of and carry out an investigation of the thermal insulator properties of different materials.

Possible sheet materials would include metal foil, plastic, felt, polystyrene, foam, bubble plastic, cotton, cotton wool, paper and card. Ask pairs or groups of learners to compare any three, four or five materials. Groups could be assigned materials to test. Ask learners to plan the test and the recording and presentation of methods. Can they explain why some materials are better thermal insulators than others? Once the results are in, ask them to group the materials and to use their evidence to explain why some materials are used in the clothing designed for very cold environments.

NC science objectives

- Plan different types of scientific enquiries to answer questions, including recognising and controlling variables where necessary (Upper Key Stage 2 working scientifically);

- Compare and group together everyday materials on the basis of their properties, including hardness, solubility, transparency, conductivity (electrical and thermal) and response to magnets (Year 5 properties and changes of materials);

- Give reasons, based on evidence from comparative and fair teats, for the particular uses of everyday materials, including metals, wood and plastic (Year 5 properties and changes of materials).

NC mathematics objectives

- Use all four operations to solve problems involving measure (for example, length, mass, volume, money) using decimal notation, including scaling (Year 5 measurement);

- Count backwards through zero to include negative numbers (Year 4 number – length, mass, volume);

- Complete, read and interpret information in tables, including timetables (Year 5 statistics).

Conclusion

Working scientifically (DfE, 2013) provides a hugely powerful link for primary teachers between science and mathematics because as learners develop their skills of working scientifically, they have to order, count, measure and examine the results of investigations in numerical forms. Science enables learners to work mathematically through the three aims of the mathematics curriculum: fluency, problem solving and reasoning (DfE, 2013). Mathematics is the language of spatial relationships, proportionality and measures. Science seeks predictability in phenomena and mathematics gives it a language to articulate relationships within natural phenomena and between the many variables scientists seek to account for. To disregard mathematics in any way would leave science much the poorer and in many cases completely unable to move forward. This would be as debilitating as engineering without mathematics – how would a bridge, computer or spacecraft be built without knowledge of shape, space, proportionality and number?

Summary of learning

In this chapter, you will have learned:

- how mathematics contributes to science and enables connections to be made between working mathematically and working scientifically;
- how mathematics learning benefits from links with science;
- to identify opportunities to use working scientifically to strengthen meaningful learning across both subjects.

10

Earth and Space

This chapter will ensure that you:

- understand that mathematics is integral to an understanding of Earth and space;

- appreciate how Earth and space provides a meaningful context for learning mathematics using, for example, large numbers.

Overview

This is an exciting topic for most primary aged learners, who tend to be very interested in the Moon, the Sun and the planets. They may not realise that the planets appear regularly in the night sky because at night the planets just look like bright stars. As teachers, this topic can be rewarding to teach. It can also present challenges, as much of what pupils are learning about cannot be observed directly. Mathematics assists learning in this area because many of the ways we talk about or describe objects in space use mathematical vocabulary or ideas. This includes measures used in both science and mathematics, for example, hours, days, kilometres, and the language of relative sizes, proportion, orientation, estimation and more.

Learners will study the Sun, Moon and Earth as approximately spherical bodies. They will need to learn about the twenty-four hour spin of the Earth on its own axis giving us day and night. You need to be sure about terms like spin, orbit, rotate and axis, and how they relate to one another. Learners will learn about the orbit of the Moon around the Earth (Figure 10.1). You can take this further by showing that the Moon continuously orbits the Earth as it travels on its 364.25 day orbit of the Sun, giving us a year. Another important feature for us on Earth

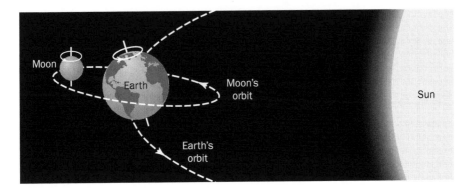

Figure 10.1 The Moon in orbit of the Earth and the Earth in orbit of the Sun. (dotted lines show the path of the orbits, labels refer to the 24 hour spin of the Earth and the 28 day orbit of Earth by the Moon and the 365.25 day orbit of the Sun by the Earth.)

is the seasons, caused by the tilt of planet Earth. Learners will study the other planets of the Solar System, their features and their orbits of the Sun (DfE, 2013).

You should develop your understanding of how the Earth, Moon and planets move in relation to one another and the Sun. Learners may ask about other things in space well beyond the National Curriculum (DfE, 2013), such as comets, meteorites and black holes. As a primary teacher, you are not expected to know all about these things but you can learn with the learners by asking them to conduct their own research (Cross and Bowden, 2014).

Teaching tip

Together with your learners, visit the Children's University of Manchester website where you will find an excellent section on 'space'. There are several sections that apply to mathematics and science, e.g. day and night. Go to http://www.childrensuniversity.manchester.ac.uk/.

An example of a scientist

Caroline Herschel (Figure 10.2) is not remembered in the same way as her very famous brother William Herschel. In 1783, William gave his sister Caroline a telescope. She immediately began to make her own observations and was soon making her own discoveries, including a number of comets and nebulae (a giant cloud of dust and gas). Her first discovery of a comet was in 1786. Like the other comets she discovered, this one is named after her, Comet C/1786 P1 (Herschel). Like all astronomers, Caroline Herschel had to take careful measurements and use a

Figure 10.2 Pencil sketch of Caroline Herschel (1750–1848)

great deal of mathematics in order to say, for example, how high a comet was in the sky night after night, and how bright the comet was as the nights of observation progressed. Caroline and William worked together for years. Caroline was his assistant but she was recognised in her own right and honoured by the Royal Astronomical Society in 1828 with a gold medal. Find out more about Caroline at www.womanastronomer.com. Other scientists you might study include Galileo, Shoemaker, Kepler and Hawking.

Connecting mathematics and science: Earth and space

Discoveries continue to be made in space, but many things we learn about space are things that we cannot see! One example is the presence of a planet orbiting a distant star. In 1998, astronomers noticed the distant star Gliese 876 swaying from side to side. Using the Hubble Space Telescope (Figure 10.3) to observe the stars swaying, they were able to use mathematics to calculate that the sway was caused by the gravitational attraction of a large planet, twice the size of Jupiter, orbiting the star. This is an example of how mathematics enables science in very powerful ways. Find out more about this and the Hubble Space Telescope at http://hubblesite.org/.

As Caroline Herschel was aware, in order to study astronomy you have to use mathematics. Mathematics and science have always been very strongly linked in the study of the planets, the Moon and outer space. When we learn about outer space, we have to learn about size, shape, distances and think in three dimensions, as the Earth, Moon, Sun and planets are almost spherical and

Figure 10.3 Hubble Space Telescope Reproduced with permission from the Office of Public Outreach at the Space Telescope Science Institute (STSci)

move in space in relation to one another. We have to imagine objects spinning on their axis and about the idea of orbit and that these spins and orbits occur at different speeds – for example, the Earth spins on its axis once every twenty-four hours, while the Moon spins much more slowly (once every twenty-eight days). Study of the Earth and space is a great opportunity for mathematics, through

Teaching tip

Create a classroom questions poster to which learners can add questions themselves. As you seek answers, stress the mathematics that will inevitably arise. For example, light from our star the Sun takes a little over nine minutes to travel the 93 million miles from the Sun to planet Earth! Divide 93 by 9 to discover how far light travels in one minute. One light minute!

areas such as number, geometry and algebra, to come alive in classrooms and for science education to reflect the reality of the world of the astronomer, the scientist of the night sky.

A real-life example with mathematics and science

Does your tablet, computer or mobile phone know your location? Do you use satnav? Your global positioning system (GPS) device takes data from orbiting satellites and collates those data to determine and tell you where you are. It can plot you on a map and remind you where to find the nearest coffee shop. Clearly, science enables this through knowledge of electricity, electronics and space flight but it also relies on computational thinking (DfE, 2013) and mathematics in dealing with and making sense of streams of data.

Key teaching points for Earth and space

As a teacher, Earth and space presents some great advantages and some challenges. Advantages are associated with the high level of interest you will encounter when learners study Earth and space. Linked to this is the sense of awe and wonder that we encounter when we consider outer space and study the things we find in outer space. The inaccessibility of outer space is of course a challenge, which means making the most of observations we can make safely and using secondary sources, illustrations, text and models. The good news is that this form of research is an important part of working scientifically (DfE, 2013). We can't take our learners directly into space but we can access reference books and some amazing internet sites (e.g. Google Earth). Using these sources of evidence also requires learners to reason, a key skill in working mathematically.

Earth and space is a rich area for mathematics through geometry and statistics related to the planets and their movement. Outer space is of course three-dimensional and demands the ability to think in three dimensions. Space is also an opportunity to explore big numbers (e.g. it is around 250,000 miles to the Moon. So how far is it there and back? How far might it be to the next nearest plant, Venus?). Using large numbers requires learners to think about numbers, to be able to have good number sense and an appreciation of place value.

Scale models are usually a concept that learners can understand, as many of their toys are models of people or objects. To learners, these are just minature versions of the real thing. Model homes, dolls, toy animals, model soldiers, etc. are very familiar to children. They can understand that a model of a person might be one-tenth the size of a real person, thus the model's clothing will also need to be one-tenth the size of real clothes. What might be new to them is the use here of the mathematical terminology of the fraction, in this case one-tenth. The next step is to use the correct proportional mathematical expression 1:9 (see Chapter 4: Proportionality).

This has implications for the teaching of working scientifically (DfE, 2013). Because learners cannot conduct tests with planets, for example, there may appear to be limited opportunity for them to carry out investigations. There are, however, several aspects of working scientifically that can be accessed, including taking readings and making comparisons, observation and using secondary sources (Table 10.1).

Teaching tip

As homework, ask the learners to draw the Moon each evening over a week or two using Table 10.2 as a framework.

Teaching tip

In order to look at the patterns in the appearance of the Moon, ask the learners to observe displays on websites such as that at http://www.moonconnection.com/moon_phases_calendar.phtml.

Table 10.1 Opportunities to develop aspects of working scientifically alongside mathematics

Element of working scientifically	Possible activity involving mathematics
Asking questions	Learners are asked to pose questions and problems about Earth and space on a blog or poster
Performing simple tests	Using model meteorites of different sizes, drop them into sand to determine the sizes of the craters formed. Measure the height dropped from, the size of the meteorite, width and depth of the crater
Grouping and classifying	Use information about the planets to group them by position, size, nature, number of moons, etc.
Making systematic observations	Keep a Moon diary over a week or more
Fair testing	Fair testing is somewhat limited in this topic. However, options exist such as investigating a combination of colour filters to be used in an astronaut's visor to reduce the very bright light in outer space. Use a light metre to quantify the reduction in light

Table 10.2 Recording chart for observations of the Moon

Night	Sunday evening	Monday evening	Tuesday evening	Wednesday evening	Thursday evening	Friday evening	Saturday evening
Week 1							
Week 2							

Teaching activities linking mathematics to science

Key Stage 1

Possible Approaches

Learners at this age often have an interest in and questions about the objects they see in the daytime and night-time sky. Unfortunately, the present English National Curriculum (DfE, 2013) does not address this topic. However, your school may choose to cover some aspects with this age range and they may crop up from time to time, such as when discussing day and night in mathematics. Try to encourage an interest in what learners observe and reinforce ideas about the Earth, Moon and Sun being very large and shaped like giant balls. Learners reading stories about travel, for example *Barnaby Bear Goes to Dublin* (Lewis, 2001), will be interested to see a globe of the Earth. Other books such as *Aliens Wear Underpants* (Freedman, 2007) may initiate discussion about space (see Chapter 4 references to art work 'Starry Night'). Encourage learners to ask questions and realise that we live on a spinning planet, which means that objects like the Sun, which are still relative to the Earth, appear to move.

Key Stage 2

Study of the Earth, Sun and Solar System offers many opportunities for science and mathematics. Learners love to learn facts about the planets, such as their order from the Sun, their relative sizes and the time it takes them (in Earth years) to orbit the Sun.

Topic: A tour of the Solar System

Activity: Planning the tour

All or part of your topic might include an itinerary for a tour of the Solar System with perhaps pages or posters about each object in the tour. Ask learners to imagine a holiday brochure for holidays in space! Could they write the brochure? Perhaps ask different learners or groups of learners to write a postcard from a planet or moon in the Solar System? Challenge them to include as much science, information and statistics as possible.

Activity: Data for the captain of the rocket

If you are going to visit the planets, it will be important to know a little about those on your itinerary (Table 10.3). Can learners complete an information sheet like that shown in Table 10.4? Or you could give them the data and ask them to identify the planet.

NC science objectives

- Record data and results of increasing complexity using scientific diagrams and labels, classification keys, tables, scatter graphs, bar and line graphs (Upper Key Stage 2 working scientifically);

- Describe the movement of the Earth, and other planets, relative to the Sun in the Solar System (Year 5 Earth and space).

NC mathematics objectives

- Read, write, order and compare numbers to at least 1,000,000 and determine the values of each digit (Year 5 number – number and place value);

- Solve number problems and practical problems that involve all of the above (very large numbers, counting in steps of powers of ten, negative numbers, rounding numbers) (Year 5 number – number and place value);

- Complete, read and interpret information in tables, including timetables (Year 5 Statistics).

Table 10.3 Information about the planets

Planet	Distance from the Sun (km)	Size (diameter) (km)	Orbit time of Sun in Earth days	Time to spin once	Number of moons
Rocky inner planets					
Mercury	58 million	5,000	88	59 Earth days	0
Venus	108 million	12,000	225	243 Earth days	0
Earth	150 million	12,500	365.25	24 Earth hours	1
Mars	228 million	5,500	687	24 Earth hours	0
Gas giants					
Jupiter	778 million	143,000	4,330	10 hours	63
Saturn	1.5 billion	120,000	10,756	10.5 hours	60
Icy outer planets					
Uranus	2.8 billion	51,000	30,687	17 hours	27
Neptune	4.5 billion	49,000	60,000	16 hours	13
Pluto (dwarf planet)	5.9 billion	2,300	90,500	6 days	3

Source: http://www.bobthealien.co.uk/table.htm

Table 10.4 Distances scaled to a model of the Solar System

Planet	Approximate distance from the Sun (km)	On a scale model this would be where 1 mm = 1,000,000 km
Mercury	58,000,000	58 mm
Venus	108,000,000	
Earth	150,000,000	
Mars	228,000,000	
Jupitor	779,000,000	
Saturn	1,426,000,000	
Uranus	2,874,000,000	
Neptune	4,500,000,000	
Pluto	5,945,000,000	

Source: Based on an idea by Feasey and Gallear (2000)

Topic: Modelling space

Activity: Models make it clear

Learners can take learning about scale further by making scale models of the Solar System or of the Moon and Earth. (See Chapter 4 for more on scale and proportionality and Chapter 6: Measurement.) Some useful options for these models are summarized below.

Earth and Moon 2-D paper plate model (not to scale)

Make a small hole in the centre of a large paper plate. On the rim of the plate stick a card disc 1 cm in diameter, shaded light grey to represent the Moon. Make a second card disc about 6 cm in diameter and shade it another colour to represent the Earth. Make a hole in the middle and use a paper fastener to fix the small Earth disc to the larger plate that holds the 'Moon' in position. Now learners can rotate the Earth disc to show the spin of the Earth and they can move the Moon around the Earth to show its orbit of the Earth.

A 3-D alternative is the orange and grape model

A simple arrangement of an orange and a grape allows a model (not to scale) to copy some of the ways the nearly spherical Earth and Moon move in relation to one another. Before you start, put a tiny blob of Blu Tack © on the 'Moon'. Then arrange the Moon in orbit around the Earth. Imagine the Blu Tack © is an astronaut who might be looking at the Earth from the Moon. If this model were roughly to scale, the grape should be approximately 150 cm from the orange. Challenge learners to make a more accurate scale model.

Scaled model of the Solar System

A scaled alternative might be constructed using the following information. A scale model of the Solar System begins with the enormous Sun scaled down to the size of a beach ball (diameter 30 cm). At this scale, the planets will be represented by balls of different sizes as follows:

Mercury would be a ball	1 mm in diameter	12 m from the Sun
Venus would be a ball	2.5 mm in diameter	33 m from the Sun
Earth would be a ball	3 mm in diameter	32 m from the Sun
Mars would be a ball	1.5 mm in diameter	49 m from the Sun
Jupiter would be a ball	30 mm in diameter	167 m from the Sun

Saturn would be a ball	26 mm in diameter	300 m from the Sun
Uranus would be a ball	10 mm in diameter	600 m from the Sun
Neptune would be a ball	10 mm in diameter	900 m from the Sun
Pluto (dwarf planet) would be a ball	1 mm in diameter	1270 m from the Sun

(Based on an activity in the ASE (1990) book *The Earth in Space*)

NC science objectives

- Recording data and results of increasing complexity using scientific diagrams and labels, classification keys, tables, scatter graphs, bar and line graphs (Upper Key Stage 2 working scientifically);

- Describe the movement of the Earth, and other Planets, relative to the Sun in the Solar System (Year 5 Earth and space);

- Describe the Sun, Earth and Moon as approximately spherical bodies (Year 5 Earth and space).

NC mathematics objectives

- Use all four operations to solve problems involving measurement using decimal notation, including scaling (Year 5 measurement);

- Identify 3-D shapes, including cubes and other cuboids, from 2-D representations (Year 5 geometry – properties of shape);

- Complete, read and interpret information in tables, including timetables (Year 5 statistics).

Topic: Explaining day and night

Activity: You are on a rotating planet

Ask two learners to model the Sun and the Earth. The head of one learner is the Sun (you could give them a dome-shaped hat labelled 'Sun'). The other learner's head is the Earth (they could wear a hat labelled 'Earth'). Ask the learner modelling Earth to look straight ahead and slowly rotate on the spot so that their eyes see the 'Sun' but then turn away. Ask the class to explain how this models the movement of the Earth relative to the Sun. You can repeat this with the child modelling the Earth facing a bright window or even (with care) a very low-powered torch. You might wish to visit http://www.ictgames.com/dayNight/. Now shift the learners' attention to data. Ask them to think about how many hours of light and dark we experience and how many times this cycle occurs each month. They can then calculate the hours of light each month.

Then challenge them with the idea that in countries away from the equator, seasons occur and day length changes. Useful times for sunset and sunrise can be obtained at the websites below.

> http://www.childrensuniversity.manchester.ac.uk/interactives/science/earthandbeyond/sunrisesunset/ provides a very accessible display

> http://academo.org/demos/day-night-terminator/ provides a more challenging display for Greenwich Meantime for any spot on Earth

Start by setting today's date and show how the daylight moves across the Earth with the hour of the day (have a torch and globe at hand to explain the shape and movement of the shadow). Note the times of sunset and sunrise and compare these to 22 December (winter solstice) and 21 June (summer solstice).

Explain that before the ideas of scientist and mathematician Nicolaus Copernicus in the 1500s, people thought the Sun orbited around the Earth. Copernicus made scientific observations of the movement of the Sun, Moon and stars and had concluded that the Sun was still and that Earth orbited the Sun. We now have masses of evidence that this is the case. However, Copernicus' ideas were rejected at the time by the church, and it was only years later that the church accepted the evidence.

NC science objectives

- Use the idea of the Earth's rotation to explain day and night and the apparent movement of the Sun across the sky (Year 5 Earth and space);

- Identify scientific evidence that has been used to support or refute ideas and arguments (Upper Key Stage 2 working scientifically).

NC mathematics objectives

- Solve number problems and practical problems that involve all of the above (Year 5 number – number and place value);

- Complete, read and interpret information in tables, including timetables (Year 5 statistics).

Conclusion

This chapter has shown how mathematics contributes to the study of the Earth and space in science. It has shown that at different stages of our understanding of space, mathematics has played an essential part. Study of Earth in space is an opportunity for learners to look at their home planet differently and to see how it moves in the Solar System and that this affects life on Earth.

Summary of learning

In this chapter, you will have learned:

- that there are clear opportunities for mathematics – particularly through geometry, numbers and statistics – and science to link to the topic of Earth and space;

- about ways in which science and mathematics are linked in the real world to this topic.

- that the language of and ideas about mathematics assist and enrich our understanding of science;

- to anticipate possible misconceptions and errors linked to Earth and space.

11

Forces

This chapter will ensure that you:

- understand that forces offers many opportunities to link mathematics and science;

- know how to help learners to perceive and begin to measure forces;

- appreciate that forces are all around us, many of which are helpful when teaching this topic;

- have a number of useful contexts to enable learners to solve problems, reason and work scientifically.

Overview

Very young learners learn about forces in the playground and when playing with their moving toys, which they push and pull. They experience movement on seesaws and scooters that results from a push, and on slides when, after gaining height, their gravitational energy pulls them down towards the ground. In school, they learn more about different forces, including friction, and their effects. They investigate forces and learn to measure them in Newtons. As a teacher, you should be aware that there are safety issues involved in stretching materials, testing, moving and dropping objects but in most cases common sense, normal classroom supervision and a warning to pupils will suffice (ASE, 2014).

There are many opportunities for mathematics in this science topic of forces, especially working mathematically, describing movement and the forces required to move objects, and how this movement is affected by forces including friction on different surfaces. Study of forces includes a wide range of experience of

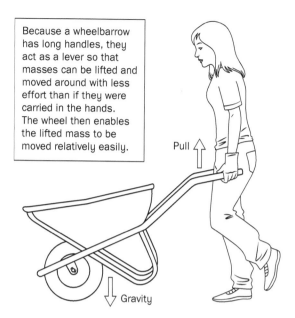

Because a wheelbarrow has long handles, they act as a lever so that masses can be lifted and moved around with less effort than if they were carried in the hands. The wheel then enables the lifted mass to be moved relatively easily.

Pull

Gravity

Figure 11.1 A wheelbarrow with force arrows and an explanation

pushing, pulling, falling objects, stretching materials, friction, air resistance and water resistance. Learners will explore springs, levers, pulleys and gears. You will need to understand a little about how these simple mechanisms can be used to change movement, including the speed of movement. A wheelbarrow acts as a lever: you pull up on the long handles and can lift objects in the barrow a little more easily than with your bare hands (Figure 11.1).

Multiple gears on bicycles can be switched to decrease or increase the force the pedals exert on the wheels. Pulleys are less common in our lives, though they are present in our washing machines where a strong belt connects a driven pulley wheel to another pulley wheel on the washing drum (Figure 11.2).

Gear wheels have teeth or cogs that mesh (Figure 11.3). A small driven gear wheel with 15 teeth might be used to drive a larger gear wheel with 30 teeth. This mathematical ratio of 15:30 can be expressed as 3:6 or 1:2. Thus the large wheel turns half as fast as the small wheel. Also note that each of the wheels turns in a different direction.

Teaching tip

Borrow a set of gears from the early years department and use a visualiser to demonstrate the action of gears to the class.

Figure 11.2 Pulley wheels allow the direction and size of force to be changed

If the small gear wheel drives the large gear wheel, the small gear wheel is the drive wheel and the large one is the driven wheel at a ratio of 15:30, which can be expressed as 3:6 or as 1:2. The small wheel will turn twice for every full turn of the large wheel, which means this arrangement will have a slowing affect. What would happen to the gear ratio if the large wheel were to becomes the drive wheel?

Figure 11.3 Two gear wheels mesh 15:30

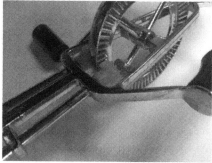

Figure 11.4 Everyday examples of gear wheels (hand drill and food whisk)

As a teacher, you should be clear about gravity as a force. This means that you need to get your head around an important distinction. In everyday speech, people talk about weight measured in kilograms and grams; however, this is wrong and weight should be measured in Newtons. Weight is relative to the place you are – that is, the planet or moon where you live. Thus your mass may be 80 kg but your weight on Earth would be close to 800 Newtons! This sounds scary, but your weight would drop to around 130 Newtons on the Moon! Kilograms and grams measure mass, which is the stuff you are made of, the matter, thus your mass remains the same wherever you are. You may need to re-read this paragraph and think about it until it becomes clear in your mind.

Magnetism is another force to be studied but is often taught separately to avoid any confusion. Though we tend not to have instruments in primary schools for measuring the force of magnetism, learners can observe its effects and gain a sense of the strength of magnetism by testing how many paper clips a magnet can lift. You should have access to a magnetic compass, the needle of which is itself a magnet. Learners can investigate how the magnetic compass reacts to a bar magnet.

Teaching tip

Ask learners to test the strength of magnets as above or by testing their strength through increasing numbers of sheets of paper or card. Go on to research the way magnets are used by utilising secondary resources (e.g. making magnet toys).

An example of a scientist

The unit of measurement of force is the Newton, which celebrates the English scientist who through his discoveries in mathematics and science changed the

Figure 11.5 Statue of Isaac Newton (1643–1727) in Grantham, Lincolnshire

world (Figure 11.5). As well as describing movement and force through his three laws of motion, he invented calculus and made discoveries about light. It is said that Newton did not attend school but developed an insatiable thirst for knowledge and most importantly began to ask questions about what he saw, such as why do objects fall to the ground? Millions of humans before him had observed falling objects but none had articulated such a useful set of explanations. While his three laws have been superseded and are not used by those studying the very, very large and the very, very small, they are still meaningful and useful to us living on the surface of planet Earth. Newton's three laws are:

1. Every object in a state of uniform motion tends to remain in that state unless an external force is applied.
2. Force = mass × acceleration.
3. For every action there is an equal and opposite reaction.

Newton understood that mathematics was key to understanding and working in the physical world; mathematics is often the natural accompanying subject to physics. Reasoning – one of the three aims of mathematics in the curriculum

Figure 11.6 By squeezing a balloon, a child reveals the size of the push force

(DfE, 2013) – was a particular skill Newton displayed. For example, if objects all fall in the same direction in predictable ways, what phenomena are responsible?

Connecting mathematics and science: forces

Younger learners will describe forces qualitatively with superlative language, including small push/pull, bigger push/pull, biggest push/pull, and so on. This and the inevitable orientation and directional language required means that these learners are using the vocabulary and ideas of mathematics immediately. If I were to push a toy car with a small force, can I predict how far will it go? Test this out with learners by measuring the distance covered on non-standard units such as carpet tiles on the floor. What was the direction? Test a second vehicle for a comparison – did it travel further? The same? Less far?

In order to allow a learner to 'feel' a force applied, use an elastic material such as the latex of a balloon to make a simple force meter (Figure 11.6). This provides a qualitative feel and view of the amount of force being applied.

Later we allow learners to measure forces quantitatively with a special force meter. Calibrated in Newtons, the Newton meter celebrates Issac Newton (Figure 11.7). Learners can make their own force meter, such as that shown in Figure 11.8. To use this second force meter, hold the cardboard tube and press the end of the dowel against objects so that the elastic band stretches a little. Learners can mark the dowel with colours to show very small push forces and other larger push forces. They can calibrate it in Newtons by pressing it against an existing Newton meter.

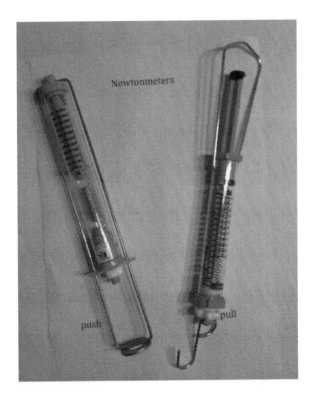

Figure 11.7 Push and pull Newton meters

A real-life example with mathematics and science

A holiday flight is a good example of mathematics and science being employed to solve a problem related to forces. The crew on the flight deck will have studied

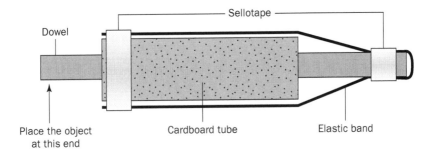

Figure 11.8 Make and calibrate your own force meter

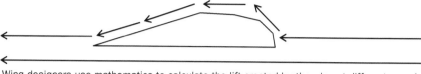

The air forced over the wing has to travel faster, reducing air pressure, effectively sucking the wing upwards (lift)

Wing designers use mathematics to calculate the lift created by the wing at different speeds

Figure 11.9 Air flow over a wing

physics related to how a plane flies, for example, how air resistance slows a plane but how the same air rushing over and below a wing creates a difference in pressure, which lifts the wing and the plane against gravity (Figure 11.9). The flight crew calculate the mass of the plane taking into account crew, passengers, fuel and luggage, and use that information together with wind speed and the characteristics of the plane to adjust the force from the engines to select a speed that will result in a safe take-off and flight.

Key teaching points for forces

This is a great topic for working scientifically and mathematically (DfE, 2013). Learners can develop all of the science skills of observation, questioning, prediction, testing, recording, concluding, and so on. It also enables the development of mathematics skills through concepts in mathematics such as the properties of shape, pattern, estimation, measures, statistics and more. Forces provide a powerful context for problem solving in mathematics and for reasoning. An example would be learners investigating a conjecture: does friction affect all surfaces that touch one another?

Simple tests can be used when comparing different forces applied to balls, sliding and rolling objects. When learners have observed the effect of stretch of two or three materials, can they then predict the effect on others? As a teacher, you should have an eye on safety when planning and supervising learners studying forces.

Teaching tip

You could visit the following useful website:

http://www.sciencekids.co.nz/videos/physics/gears.html

Teaching activities linking mathematics to science

Key Stage 1

Possible Approaches

Forces are not included in the curriculum for science (DfE, 2013) at Key Stage 1. However, learners in EYFS are likely to explore forces in toys and playgrounds, and forces will of course be experienced by 5–7 year olds. In traditional stories such as 'Jack and the Beanstalk' (Treahy, 2012) and 'Winne the Pooh' (Milne, 1926), much of the action revolves around movement of objects and so involves forces. Forces feature when objects are pushed, pulled and blown (Figure 11.10). You will be able to discuss learners' ideas about forces and suggest simple safe activities.

Figure 11.10 Learners feel and observe the forces in a push of war!

Key Stage 2

Topic: Fireman Sam's car

Activity: Testing surfaces for a vehicle

Introduce the activity with a video or story about Fireman Sam or another character. Explain that learners are to investigate different forces and how they affect a car. This could involve different pushes to cars on a range of surfaces, testing vehicles with different numbers of wheels, and trialling wheels made from or covered in different materials. Learners might test a vehicle carrying progressively greater loads (masses).

Arrange a slope for the learners to play with and observe different toy cars rolling down the slope and then travelling over a surface. Ask them to plan how they might test other surfaces to see which is the best or worst surface for a car to travel over. Can they make a prediction and then design a simple test or, better, a fair test?

NC science objectives

- Ask relevant questions and use different types of scientific enquiries to answer them (Lower Key Stage 2 working scientifically);
- Compare how things move on different surfaces (Year 3 forces and magnets).

NC mathematics objectives

- Measure, compare and subtract – lengths (Year 3 measurement);
- Interpret and present data using bar charts, pictograms and tables (Year 3 statistics).

Topic: Return of space mission

Activity: Parachutes for the spacecraft's return to Earth

Introduce a planned space flight to Mars and the need to land safely back on Earth. The capsule will slow from many thousands of kilometres an hour to a very gentle landing. Parachutes will facilitate this, so we need good parachutes. Ask groups of learners to evaluate different shapes, sizes, materials, numbers and lengths of strings so that the class determines the best arrangement for parachutes. Allow them all to make a mini parachute and check they know about payload, strings and canopy.

NC science objectives

- Use test results to make predictions to set up further comparative and fair tests (Upper Key Stage 2 working scientifically);

- Identify the effects of air resistance, water resistance and friction, which act between moving surfaces (Year 5 forces).

NC mathematics objectives

- Use all four operations to solve problems involving measure using decimal notation, including scaling (Year 5 measurement);

- Calculate and interpret the mean as an average (Year 6 statistics).

Table 11.1 Others contexts for use of forces in mathematics and science

Context	Forces involved	Mathematics and science
Grippy shoes	pull, friction	Measure the force required to pull the shoe
Pulleys and gears	push, friction	Count the turns of the drive wheel and of the wheel that is driven
Windmills, parachutes	push, pull, air resistance	Measure surface area and sail speed, e.g. number of spins each 30 seconds or seconds to land on the ground
Ballistas	pushes and air resistance	Use a pull force meter to measure the push of the ballista. Measure the effect of air resistance on the distance travelled
Skateboards	push, pull, friction, air resistance	Measure the pull or push required to move the skateboard over different surfaces
Water wheel	push, pull, gravity, water resistance	Count the spins of the wheel in 60 seconds under a running tap on different settings

Conclusion

Forces are an interesting, exciting and fun aspect of science for learners. This is because forces are about the real world, about movement and about the things that learners encounter in their daily lives. Forces allow learners to handle materials and make real measurements. They provide great opportunities to reinforce learning about mathematics in the real world and working scientifically and mathematically. Both ways of working provide opportunities to motivate and challenge learners. Patterns can emerge as can the need to repeat a test. Errors also occur but again provide learning opportunities. In fact, it is often mathematics that reveals an experimental error when anomalous readings are observed.

Summary of learning

In this chapter, you will have learned:

- about the many simple contexts that allow us to learn about forces and that mathematics and science work well together here;
- about the importance of seeing and feeling forces for primary learners;
- how to measure forces numerically;
- that although safety is paramount, learners should not be prevented from handling objects and measuring forces;
- that many of the forces experienced in daily life are useful in mathematics and science classes, e.g. gravity, friction, air resistance, water resistance.

12

Electricity

This chapter will ensure that you:

- have an appreciation of those areas where mathematics can contribute to the study of electricity in primary education;
- are aware of real-life contexts that assist learning about electricity in connection with learning mathematics.

Overview

Making and investigating simple circuits is for some learners a high point in primary science. It is something they enjoy, something they find intriguing and almost always remember. Most primary learners find the whole topic of electricity enjoyable. However, considering the title of this book, there are perhaps fewer links with mathematics at the primary level than you might think. Electricity, though, has a lot to offer in terms of learner motivation and links to the real world, which almost always uses mathematics. Electricity is a form of energy alongside light energy and sound energy, and so the theme of energy is a basis for strong links within science. Study of electricity at the primary level can be exploited for links with mathematics, such as exploring whether increased voltage leads to a buzzer making more noise.

An example of a real scientist

Michael Faraday (1791–1867) was an English scientist who is credited with the discovery of electricity (Figure 12.1). In fact, electricity was known about before Faraday but it was seen as a curiosity. His work on electromagnetic induction

Figure 12.1 Photograph of Michael Faraday (1791–1867) Reproduced with the permission of the Wellcome Library, London

meant that electricity could be generated and used in ways we now take for granted. Faraday himself was not a great mathematician but he is credited with inspiring others who used his ideas alongside mathematics to extend understanding further. He made other discoveries and was recognised in many ways for his brilliance, including giving the very first Christmas lecture on science at the Royal Institute in London in 1826. Find more about his life and work at http://www.rigb.org/our-history/michael-faraday.

Teaching tip

Allow learners to connect components in a circuit driven by one 1.5 volt cell. They will see that some components work [depending on whether the bulb is labelled (rated) 1.5 V, 2.5 V, 6 V, etc.], some don't work and some don't work well. Allow them to increase the voltage to 3 V by wiring in another 1.5 V cell (taking care to wire the two cells – to + (getting this wrong is not dangerous, it just won't work!). Can they predict the effect? What do they observe? Take care with this, as bulbs rated 1.5 V will be blown by a 6 V battery (this is not dangerous just wasteful, the term 'blown' referring to the very quick and bright burn out of the tiny filament of the bulb). Ask learners how they have used science and mathematics.

Connecting mathematics and science: electricity

Observation and classification are two skills of this topic that link to mathematics and science the strongest. Learners can observe electrical components and their uses. These can be categorised and grouped. Which electrical components make light? Which electrical components make a sound? Which make movement? Are some used in the home?

The National Curriculum in England (DfE, 2013) does not require measurement of electricity in primary education, but measurement of amperage (current) in a circuit is a very useful extension activity and does allow quantitative measure of current when we change the flow of electricity. Amps are a measure of the current – that is, the number of electrons travelling around the circuit. We can teach about volts in primary science but generally we don't measure voltage beyond adding the voltage of each cell we combine in a circuit. In a circuit we seek balance; that is, a 3 V battery will drive 3 V components. If using a 4.5 V bulb, we could connect three 1.5 V cells to make a 4.5 V battery. Note that when using a single 1.5 V cell, the amperage will be around 0.5 of one amp.

Teaching tip

A simple way to classify electrical devices is to sketch a plan of a home with the rooms labelled (e.g. kitchen, bedroom, bathroom). Learners can cut out pictures of devices from a catalogue, sketch items or just create name labels that they can then arrange grouped within the different rooms. There will be lots of opportunities to discuss items used in more than one room and of course safety issues, for example, why are so few devices used in the bathroom?

A real-life example with mathematics and science

More and more homes and schools are installing photovoltaic panels on the roof. Many of us will have considered whether this is financially worthwhile. This requires some straightforward mathematics and an appreciation of some of the science involved. How much electricity does the household use? How much would the panels generate? What would be the saving on the cost of electricity? What might I receive in terms of a subsidy? Learners might be asked to carry out these calculations for the school based on the school's electricity bill for the last quarter. Where a home or school has photovoltaic panels installed, it should be possible for learners to monitor the production of electricity over a day and on different days, so that the effect of the weather or even day length can be observed (Table 12.1).

Table 12.1 Table of electrical generation on different days

Day	Monday	Tuesday	Wednesday	Thursday	Friday
Time					
Weather					
Output					

Key teaching points for electricity

As with other science topics, vocabulary is important and as learners and teachers are perhaps less than familiar with electrical terms, we advise care. Electricity is an invisible form of energy and this is a little abstract, so learners may see it as rather mysterious and magical. It is neither, it is simply a natural phenomenon that we discovered and have learned to harness. As teachers, we need to be aware of this and that some ideas are counter-intuitive (e.g. the flow of electricity can be likened to the flow of water but that water analogies for electricity are not really acceptable!). The SPACE report on electricity provides useful insights into learners' ideas about electricity (see Osborne et al., 1991).

Learners will have seen electrical appliances and should be taught about them and about basic electrical safety. They will be keen to use electrical appliances and plugs but young learners should be warned about the danger and should not be allowed to handle plugs and mains-powered appliances in school. You might want to talk about how mains electricity is made in power stations, often from coal, gas or oil. Learners will be aware of electricity pylons and cables but may not have made the link to the sockets on the wall. Learners may be amazed to hear about 150 000 V cables above their heads! Again, they should be warned to keep away from equipment that is part of the national electrical grid. See safety advice and activities at www.powerdiscoveryzone. com.

Learners can find out about electricity from books and from websites. Such resources can reinforce learning but should not be used to replace opportunities to handle and use real electrical components. In these books, learners will find reference to mathematical ideas through numbers, classification, observation and measurement.

Readers may know that there is a link between electricity and magnetism. When first teaching about them, it is advantageous to avoid confusion and teach them separately. However, using a magnetic compass, learners can observe a magnetic effect from electrical components in use. In the later primary years, we can show learners how to make and use an electromagnet.

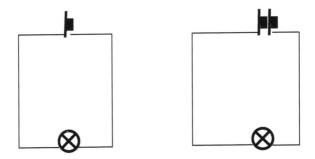

Figure 12.2 Two different circuits: which bulb will be brightest?

Teaching tip

Ask learners to build a circuit including wire, one cell and one bulb. Ask them to demonstrate the circuit and then discuss ways in which they could vary the brightness of the bulb (Figure 12.2). Note whether learners mention varying the number of bulbs and/or cells. Point out that two 1.5 V cells wired together makes a 3 V battery (of cells) and three 1.5 V cells wired together make a 4.5 V battery. If learners refer to the length of the wire, explain that very, very long wires would have more resistance and would reduce the flow of electrons and have an effect.

Teaching activities linking mathematics to science

Key Stage 1

Possible Approaches

In the English National Curriculum (DfE, 2013) electricity does not feature in Key Stage 1. This means that those learners who found electricity exciting and interesting in EYFS may not be taught about electricity until lower Key Stage 2. Key Stage One teachers will find learners very interested in electricity and as a minimum should teach about basic electrical safety (e.g. only adults should deal with sockets, plugs and electrical devices). Questions about electricity will however arise, you should be willing to talk about electricity and encourage learners to read relevant non fiction books about electricity. There are also simple circuit building activities which you could include at Key Stage 1 such as making a circuit with a bulb, another with a buzzer and one perhaps with a motor. You might stress the organisation of a circuit and the match in voltage required between the cell/s and the bulbs. Simple games like this can be useful at http://www.ictgames.com/electricity.html.

Key Stage 2

Topic: Electrical safety in the home

Activity: Keeping safe with electricity

A useful initial approach with any age group is to examine the electrical devices in the home or around school. Stress the danger of mains electricity at 240 volts and use resources to enable learners to spot potential dangers around the home. You might explain that in class we use batteries of 1.5 V, 3 V, and 9 V and so the current used is not dangerous.

Learners might make a simple circuit with a cell and bulb. After checking that a circuit works disconnect one wire creating a gap in the circuit. This gap can then be bridged with different materials to see if they are electrical conductors or not. Learners can then construct two groups of materials, electrical conductors and not electrical conductors. Can learners establish a rule or conjecture about which materials conduct electricity? For example, is it all metals which conduct electricity?

An extension to this would see you asking learners to construct homes with shoe boxes. Can they now make circuits with bulbs to light the homes? Ask them to add an extra cell to the circuit first predicting what will be the affect? Ask them how they could measure the amount of light produced by a bulb or pair of bulbs (using a light meter (best done in a darkened area)). Can learners try out different combinations of bulbs and cells predicting and noting the results?

NC science objectives

- Set up simple practical enquiries, comparative and fair tests (Lower Key Stage 2 working scientifically);
- Gather, record, classify and present data in a variety of ways to help in answering questions (Lower Key Stage 2 working scientifically);
- Identify common appliances that run on electricity (Year 4 electricity);
- Construct a simple series electrical circuit, identifying and naming its basic parts, including cells, wires, bulbs, switches and buzzers (Year 4 electricity);
- Recognise that a switch opens and closes a circuit and associate this with whether or not a lamp lights in a simple series circuit (Year 4 electricity).

NC mathematics objectives

- Interpret and present discrete and continuous data using appropriate graphical methods, including bar charts and time graphs (Year 4 statistics);
- Solve comparison, sum and difference problems using information presented in bar charts, pictograms, tables and other graphs (Year 4 statistics).

Topic: Making our own components

Activity: Making an electromagnet

Make an electromagnet by winding a wire around a steel nail 30–50 times. Connect the ends of the wire to the terminals of a 1.5 V cell and observe that the nail will now pick up paper clips. You have made an electromagnet just like those used in automatic locks on doors and in many other electrical devices. Challenge learners by varying the strength of the magnet with different voltages (Figure 12.3).

NC science objectives

- Take measurements, using a range of scientific equipment, with increasing accuracy and precision, taking repeat readings when appropriate (Upper Key Stage 2 working scientifically);
- Report and present findings from enquiries, including conclusions, causal relationships, and explanations of and degree of trust in results, in oral and written forms such as displays and other presentations (Upper Key Stage 2 working scientifically);
- Compare and give reasons for variations in how components function, including the brightness of bulbs, the loudness of buzzers and the on/off position of switches (Year 6 electricity).

NC mathematics objectives

- Use all four operations to solve problems involving measure (e.g. using length, mass, volume, money) using decimal notation, including scaling (Year 5 measurement).

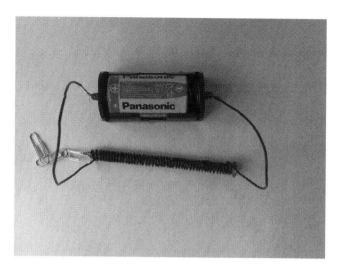

Figure 12.3 Device for testing the strength of an electromagnet

Conclusion

Electricity can be an exciting and stimulating topic in primary science with some links to mathematics. Links with mathematics are in fact very strong indeed, as any electrician will tell you, but at the primary level we are concerned with some of the ways electricity is used in the world and simple circuit building. Teaching about safety is a priority but electricity can spur a real interest in the world and in science.

Summary of learning

In this chapter, you will have learned:

- that electricity is a motivating part of science for primary pupils;
- that there are opportunities to link science and mathematics based on the study of electricity but that as the links are less numerous than in other science topics, these need to be planned for.

13

Sound and Light

This chapter will ensure that you:

- appreciate the opportunities for mathematics to contribute to learning about the science of light and sound;
- know about a range of possible investigations linking science and mathematics;
- are aware of practical and safety issues linked to the topic of light and sound.

Overview

Energy is an important theme in science. Sound and light energy are perhaps the most familiar forms of energy that learners interact with on a day-to-day basis. Both areas enable strong links between mathematics and science, such as when we measure the intensity of light and the volume of sound from different sources. Learners will explore sound and light sources, how light and sound travel, as well as about shadows, reflections and the link between vibrations and the volume of sound produced.

An example of a scientist

Thomas Alva Edison (1847–1931) was an inventor, scientist and technologist (Figure 13.1). He had a truly curious and inventive mind. As well as many other things, he invented a usable electric light bulb, a way to record sound and a form of motion picture. One of his earliest sound recordings was made onto tin foil and can be heard at http://www.scpr.org/blogs/news/2012/10/25/10712/hear-thomas-edison-sing-rare-1878-audio-restored-f/.

Figure 13.1 Photograph of Thomas Alva Edison (1847–1931)

This 137-year-old recording was made in 1878 in a museum in St. Louis, Missouri. Edison was successful partly because he used systematic testing, which we recognise as the scientific method. Edison recruited a celebrated team in his 'invention factory', including Thomas Upton whose knowledge of physics and mathematics assisted Edison greatly when tackling the improvement of the light bulb filament. Find more information at http://www.thomasedison.com/biography.html.

Connecting mathematics and science: sound and light

The youngest learners can carry out tests with sound and light making simple qualitative judgements about the magnitude of a sound or the brightness of a light. These might include:

- Which torch is brightest?
- How dark is it in our tent?
- Are bigger candles always brighter?
- Which sounds do we like?
- How far away can we hear a clock?
- Can we make ear defenders for the bear who can't get to sleep?

Teaching tip
Free decibel and light meter apps are available for tablets and phones (Figure 13.2).

Figure 13.2 Screenshot from Decibell 10th, a free app by skypaw.com

Later in the primary years, you can introduce light meters and decibel meters so that learners can measure light and sound in lux (lx) and decibels (dB) respectively (Figure 13.3). These devices or a data logger will allow quantitative measurement and the utilization of mathematics to address the following questions:

- How much light passes through these materials?
- Which torch is brightest?
- If I add a cell to the circuit, how much brighter does the bulb glow?
- How much light is reflected from these surfaces?
- What is the loudest sound in school?
- Which material is the best sound insulator?
- What is the noisiest place in school?
- When the door bell rings, how far does the sound travel?

These devices, which involve the measurement of light and sound, really do offer strong links between science and mathematics through measurement and use of statistics. There are of course other links such as the grouping and classification of sound and light sources and the study of the speed of light and sound, although

Figure 13.3 Light meters and decibel meters provide numerical data

the latter applies more to high school science. When testing with light and sound, remember to stress safety with learners; they should not expose their ears or eyes to too much sound or light.

A real-life example with mathematics and science

Most television, film and stage performances require lighting and sound. The engineers who work on stage and screen have a good understanding of light and sound, which allows them to make the very best of the stage or setting for the performance. Those who have witnessed a play where poor acoustics mean that actors cannot be heard clearly will appreciate the value of good sound engineering. In the same way that we see the creative use of lighting in a performance, learners can come to appreciate that the science and mathematics of lighting can make inanimate objects come to life. An example is the famous Symphony of Lights show in Hong Kong Harbour where each night lights and lasers illuminate the night sky and Victoria Harbour in a dazzling show. Pattern appears in the light and music, both media being accessible to young learners.

Key teaching points for sound and light

Sound and light are two accessible aspects of science that link strongly to mathematics. As well as aspects of safety, primary teachers cover the interesting phenomena of light and sound propagation, transmission, reflection and uses in the real world. It is very useful to have decibel and light meters to hand and if possible more than one design of each, so that learners can become familiar with them, their use and the units of measurement. This is a great context for learners to experience the power of measurement and number in science.

Primary classrooms can present some difficulties when teaching light and sound. When studying light in many classrooms, we encounter a problem with blackout – that is, creating a darkened area to see shadows and beams of light, etc. Similarly, when studying sound, learners can struggle with background noise. This can make reading a decibel meter very difficult. Both issues can usually be solved with a little thought and creativity. Often the learners themselves will have excellent suggestions of how to overcome these problems.

In earlier chapters we referred to data loggers, which allow learners to measure temperature, light and sound (Figure 13.4). Data loggers are accurate and provide a digital numerical readout of instances or real-time recording of measurements (Figures 13.5 and 13.6). Patterns in data encourage learners to hypothesise and conjecture.

Teaching tip

You should warn learners of the danger to their eyes and ears of exposure to very bright light and very loud sounds respectively.

If there are learners in the class with sensory impairment of sight or hearing, it is usually possible to turn this to the learners' advantage. Learners with poor hearing can be very sensitive to sound and particularly vibration. If a child

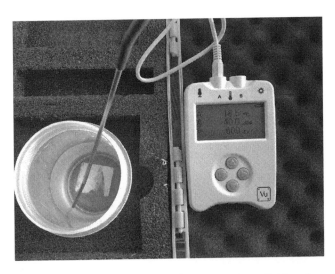

Figure 13.4 Data loggers provide readings for temperature, light and sound

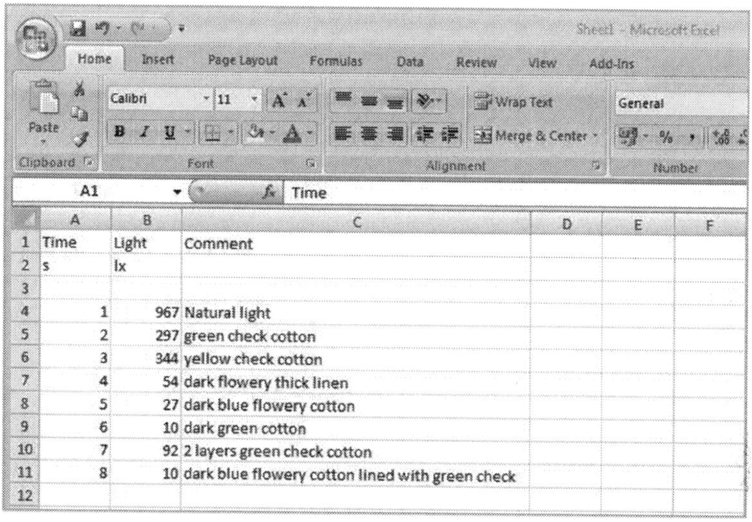

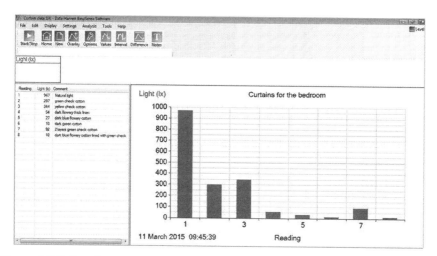

Figure 13.5 Readings from a data logger downloaded into Excel about the opacity of different fabrics (Reproduced with permission from Data Harvest Group (http://www.data-harvest.co.uk/catalogue/science/primary/datalogging/primary-vu-data-logger/2300PK))

routinely wears a microphone in class, he or she may be able to hear things in ways that others cannot, for example, carefully placing the microphone inside a guitar so that the child can report on the sound of a guitar from the inside!

Figure 13.6 Bar chart representing data about the opacity of fabrics (Reproduced with permission from Data Harvest Group (http://www.data-harvest.co.uk/catalogue/science/primary/datalogging))

Teaching activities linking mathematics to science

Key Stage 1

Possible Approaches

Light and sound do not appear in the English National Curriculum (DfE, 2013) for Key Stage 1. Learners will study light and sound in EYFS but will not study it again until Key Stage 2. However, questions about light and sound will crop up in other subjects (e.g. design and technology and art), in learners' literature and other things they come across in the world. You should be ready to deal with their questions but avoiding a simple response. Use the opportunity to make them think. For example, ask them: What do you think? Have you seen that before? How could we find out?

As a school you might decide to provide some activities on light and sound linked to the science programme of study (e.g. describe the simple physical properties of a variety of everyday materials (Year 1)). A lesson that aims to achieve this objective could ask learners to divide materials into 'see-through materials' and materials we cannot see through (transparent and opaque). One test of transparency is to try to read the book through the material or trying to shine a torch through the materials. With Key Stage 1 learners, we would judge the materials qualitatively and perhaps rank order the materials in terms of their transparency (with older learners, we could use a light meter to measure the light passing through different materials). This type of activity naturally draws on reasoning skills, one of the three aims of the mathematics curriculum (DfE, 2013).

Other parts of the Programme of Study (DfE, 2013) that involve light and sound include:

- Compare and group together a variety of everyday materials on the basis of their simple physical properties (Year 1 materials);

- Observe changes across the four seasons (Year 1 seasonal changes);

- Find out about and describe how plants need water, light and a suitable temperature to grow and stay healthy (Year 2 plants);

- Find out about and describe the basic needs of animals, including humans, for survival (water, food, air) (Year 2 animals, including humans).

Such work provides many opportunities to link to mathematics through number, simple pictograms, tally charts, block diagrams and simple tables (Year 2).

Key Stage 2: Light

Learners love making shadows, changing objects and their shadows, casting shadows from one person's silhouette while another sketches the silhouette on the wall.

Topic: Creating shadows

Activity: Patterns in shadow size

A good light source, an object that will cast a shadow, a tape measure and a screen provide the ingredients for classic, high-quality primary science. Ask a learner to hold the object and another learner to measure the distance from the object to the projector and the size of the shadow. Note these numbers and ask the learners to predict what will happen to the shadow if you move the object towards the light source. At the new position, ask a learner to measure again the distance to the light source and the size of the shadow. Discuss what happened and ask the class to formulate a science question and then design a set of tests to go about answering it. For example, when we move the object, what happens to the size of the shadow? Now ask the class in pairs to design a set of tests to answer that question. Ask them to predict the result before conducting tests and recording the results. Ideally have them design the recording sheet. When learners have their results, ask them to transfer these to a line graph. Does the shape of the graph correspond with the prediction?

NC science objectives

- Use results to draw simple conclusions (Lower Key Stage 2 working scientifically);
- Find patterns in the way that the size of a shadow changes (Year 3 light).

NC mathematics objectives

- Solve number and practical problems involving these ideas (multiples, place value; read, write, compare and order numbers to 1000;

identify, represent and estimate numbers) (Year 3 number – number and place value);

- Interpret and present data using bar charts, pictograms and tables (Year 3 statistics);
- Recognise the place value of each digit in a three-digit number (hundreds, tens, units) (Year 3 number – number and place value).

Topic: Looking after ourselves

Activity: Which fabric makes the best curtains?

Ask learners about the features of great bedroom curtains and agree that stopping light (opacity) is a key feature. Encourage them to talk about how light travels from a source to our eyes unless blocked by an opaque material. Extend this thinking by asking them to imagine we work in a curtain factory and we want to test fabrics to see if they stop the light. Can they suggest ideas about how we could do that? If they have never used a light meter, then demonstrate its use and allow learners to handle it (perhaps do a simple pre activity measuring light in different places in the classroom or school). Teach them or remind them that the unit of measurement is lux, which is a scale from 0 to 3000 lux, where 0 lux is darkness (no light) and 3000 lux is dangerously bright light (remind them never to look directly at a very bright light source such as the Sun). Now ask them to plan, predict the result of and carry out tests of fabrics to determine a good fabric for bedroom curtains.

NC science objectives

- Record data and results of increasing complexity using scientific diagrams and labels, classification keys, tables, scatter graphs, bar and line graphs (Upper Key Stage 2 working scientifically);
- Report and present findings from enquiries, including conclusions, causal relationships, explanations of and degree of trust in results, in oral and written forms such as displays and other presentations (Upper Key Stage 2 working scientifically);
- Use the idea that light travels in straight lines to explain that objects are seen because they give out light or reflect light into the eye (Year 6 light).

Key Stage 2: Sound

Topic: Vibrations make sound

Activity: Altering the pitch of sound

For this activity, learners need access to a range of tuning forks or other objects that will produce a range of pitches, such as identical bottles each containing a different amount of water, different lengths of similar plastic straws, strings on a guitar, keys on a xylophone or glokenspiel. You might show a video of vibration such as that available at http://blogs.plos.org/thestudentblog/2011/08/04/the-beat-of-the-scientific-drum/.

Ask the learners to arrange the set of objects and then blow on them or strike them to make a sound (or on tuned instruments a note). Can they describe the sound they have made? Ask them to copy the sounds with a la or whistle. Can they arrange any sounds in order of pitch – high to low or vice versa? Do they know the word pitch? Can someone explain the meaning of pitch? Can they give examples?

Introduce the word vibrate. Can they see any vibration? If not, can they feel it? If it is hard to see the vibration, gently place an inflated balloon or other hollow object on the vibrating object. What do they observe? Can they explain this? Ask them to describe the different objects and what it is that varies in the objects to produce the different sounds (e.g. in the bottles of water and straws it is the column of air that vibrates to make the sound). Can they measure the length of the vibrating materials and note a description of the pitch? Can they present this in a bar chart?

NC science objectives

- Make systematic and careful observations and, where appropriate, take accurate measurements using standard units, using a range of equipment, including thermometers and data loggers (Lower key Stage 2 working scientifically);

- Find patterns between the pitch of a sound and features of the object that produced it (Year 4 sound).

NC mathematics objectives

- Estimate, compare and calculate different measures, including money in pounds and pence (Year 4 measurement);
- Interpret and present discrete and continuous data using appropriate graphical methods, including bar charts and time graphs (Year 4 statistics).

Topic: Vibrations make sound

Activity: Altering the volume!

Musical instruments are ideal here but the lesson could be very noisy! Ask a learner to demonstrate beating gently on a drum. Ask learners to observe what happens with eyes open and again with eyes closed. Ask a learner to describe what happens when a beat is made (encourage reference to the force of the beater hitting the skin, the vibration of the skin, the vibration of the air inside the drum, the vibration of the body of the drum, that the shape of the drum makes the sound and makes the sound bigger, that the sound continues slightly). Try leading a discussion about the force of the beat being converted into sound energy. At this point, introduce a sound meter to measure the volume of the sound. Because a drum beat is of short duration, this will be more difficult. If you have a decibel meter or a decibel meter app, display it through the class visualiser. Alternatively, use a data logger.

Ask learners to plan, predict the results of and carry out tests to determine how the size of the force of beat, pluck or blow affects the volume of the sound made. When it come to testing, you may have to control the noise in the room so that tests are conducted free of ambient or other sound!

NC science objectives

- Gather, record, classify and present data in a variety of ways to help in answering questions (Lower Key Stage 2 working scientifically);

- Use results to draw simple conclusions, make predictions for new values, suggest improvements and raise further questions (Lower Key Stage 2 working scientifically);
- Find patterns between the volume of a sound and the strength of the vibrations that produced it (Year 4 sound).

NC mathematics objectives

- Estimate, compare and calculate different measures, including money in pounds and pence (Year 4 measurement);
- Interpret and present discrete and continuous data using appropriate graphical methods, including bar charts and time graphs (Year 4 statistics).

Conclusion

Sound and light are two topics that allow learners to investigate the world around them and use mathematics to order and quantify their observations. We all too readily take both light and sound for granted because they are so familiar, so it may be necessary in lessons to model the kind of questioning that enables scientific working. The familiarity of these areas of science makes them feel accessible but there are aspects like the way light travels to our eyes which is not perhaps intuitive. Mathematics and science work well together here, allowing learners to look at the familiar from a different standpoint and perhaps appreciate links and patterns that might otherwise go unnoticed.

Summary of learning

In this chapter, you will have learned:

- that many science investigations of light and sound involve mathematics;
- that the two phenomena are very familiar to learners but both have the capacity to delight and encourage curiosity;
- about the need to measure light and sound using scientific measures;
- about the need to teach about safety and care of ears and eyes;
- that some classroom tasks require low light and low sound when conducting tests.

14

Materials

This chapter will ensure that you:

- appreciate the considerable scope of the topic of materials for both science and mathematics;

- understand that science and mathematical skills can develop strongly in this part of science;

- develop leaners' knowledge and understanding through meaningful investigations and tasks in the real world of materials.

Overview

This topic often begins with observation – what learners can tell you about different materials by simply looking at them (Figure 14.1). You could reveal more detail through magnification of the materials (by 10×, 100×, 1000×, etc.). Find out more at http://www.strangematterexhibit.com/jump.html; select the option 'Fun Stuff' and then 'Zoom!'.

Figure 14.1 Children can learn by observing different materials

Figure 14.2 Stephanie Kwoleck invented Kevlar®, which is used to make armoured vests, skis, helmets and much more

An example of a scientist

Marie Curie is one of the most famous materials scientists. Another such female scientist is an American chemist. Although less well known, you will likely have benefitted from her invention on more than one occasion. Very strong and light, Kevlar® now forms a part of mobile phones, cars, ropes, canoes, sports equipment including cycles, and much more. Invented by Stephanie Kwoleck, it is used around the world and, of course, in space! She had been trialling materials that could be used as an alternative to oil-derived plastics. This new material intrigued her and she persuaded a colleague to try spinning a thread. They were amazed at its strength – it was stronger than nylon – and soon realised its potential.

Connecting mathematics and science: materials

An important aspect of science, materials science is about knowing the characteristics of materials and using this knowledge to create more and better materials. To do this, scientists use mathematics to measure quantities very carefully and to make observations and measurements about how materials perform (e.g. keep things warm or protect things). You may be interested to read about children's misconceptions of this aspect of science at http://www.nuffieldfoundation. org/primary-science-and-space/materials.

Within the topic of materials, learners have the opportunity to use number and measures (see Figure 14.3). Different tasks allow the following to be measured: length, mass, temperature, sound, force and light. These measures allow us to quantify such characteristics as:

Figure 14.3 Writing about science in Year 6 utilises mathematical notation

- roughness by touching materials with our skin;
- strength of paper using a force meter;
- elasticity by stretching elastic or another material with masses or a force meter;
- pliability (bendiness) of materials using masses or a force meter;
- hardness of materials using a scratch (steel nail) test;
- thermal conductivity using a thermometer;
- opacity/transparency using a light meter;
- water absorption and waterproofing characteristics using a measuring cylinder.

With quantitative data, we can record and present results as tables and graphs, look for pattern, consider extrapolation and interpolation, and use our evidence to answer questions and provide explanations that draw both on science and our results. And if we don't have measuring equipment, we can do much of this based on observation and description of the materials and their behaviour, such as the way materials respond to magnets.

Examples of straightforward enquiries

1   Test fabric for elasticity. Apply a pulling force to samples of materials with a force meter or Newton meter. This would allow you, for example, to see what force is required to stretch a material by 1 cm?

2   Test sheet materials (paper, card, plastic, foil, etc.) for strength. Drop a large nail down a card tube onto the material to observe the damage inflicted. You could test the affect of dropping the nail from different heights.

3   Test various papers for durability. Rub each paper with sandpaper and count the number of rubs required to make a hole in it. How could this be made a fair test?

4   Test sheet materials for thermal conductivity (e.g. different foams and silver foil) to determine whether they keep an object warm over fifteen minutes. Which material keeps things warm longest?

In each case, learners can use different measures (length, time, force, temperature) and mathematics to help them explore and investigate materials and their properties. Our human world is full of questions related to materials that we could investigate. Which paper is strongest? Which liquid is runniest? Which glue sets quickest? Which fabric keeps things warmest/coolest? Which surface produces least friction? Which material is most opaque?

A big part of primary materials involves changes to materials. Materials can be changed by heating them (e.g. egg white), by bending, stretching, twisting or squashing them (e.g. rock formations over time – heat and pressure also play a part), or by combining or mixing them with other materials (e.g. in cooking). In primary classes, start with observation and description of materials, then test and investigate materials to better describe the characteristics of the materials, and finally examine the way materials can be changed. This is not a strict order but is a useful way to summarise important aspects of the study of materials in primary schools.

A real-life example with mathematics and science

The new spacecraft Orion is planned to take NASA astronauts to Mars. For this project, materials need to be developed and new versions of combinations of materials tested. For example, in order to get back to the surface of the Earth, the command capsule will need a heat shield made of heat-resistant tiles. The tiles used on the old space shuttle were made of materials that produced pollutants when they burned up on re-entry. New tiles have been developed that protect both the command capsule and the Earth's atmosphere. Making the materials required precise measurements of the materials being mixed and tested. Tests then exposed the materials to different temperatures to determine whether they were suitable for the capsule's heat shield.

> ## Teaching tip
>
> Most learners appreciate the need to protect our ears in some environ-ments with ear defenders. A straightforward comparative test uses a radio set at a volume just above normal speech and a decibel metre held 10cm from the radio's speaker. In otherwise quiet conditions, measure the volume of the radio in decibels. Repeat this test but hold-ing different materials over the decibel meter's sensor. You could predict which of the following will reduce the sound most prior to testing and look carefully at the results: foil, cotton wool, bubble plastic, paper, cot-ton fabric, paper towel, cardboard, felt fabric, wood, etc.

Key teaching points for materials

Many of the characteristics of materials are measured with units we are unfamiliar with (e.g. energy is measured in joules, not a unit used in primary science). How-ever, we can measure some forms of energy, including heat (degrees centigrade), light (lux) and sound (decibels). One simple objective of science and mathematics is to ensure children know, use and become familiar with an increasing range of measures and make use of them!

The great news for us as teachers is that there are so many options here for science and mathematics. Materials science presents opportunities to measure things such as light, sound, force and temperature that some learners just don't do enough of. As we highlighted in Chapter 1, it is important to have older primary learners construct line graphs. We have identified a number of investigations that will produce line graphs; however, there are many more tasks that will produce block graphs. We would encourage you and your learners to collect data so that a range of graphs can be drawn, but with older learners you should seek to deal more often with line graphs.

Would any of the following lead to the production of line graphs?

- How does the rate of cooling change in different volumes of warm water?
- What is the distance a ball will travel over different surfaces?
- What is the amount of light that will travel through different materials?
- What is the amount of water absorbed by different rocks?

Only the first will produce a line graph. What about the following?

1   Test thickness of insulation for thermal insulation with layers of felt measured in millimetres and the time it takes for the temperature to drop 5°C.

2   Test the sound insulation afforded by different thicknesses of felt measured in millimetres.

3   Examine the amount of light passing through a material and the distance we can read text through that material.

4   Another option with light is to wrap a bulb in a different number of layers of a material and measure the light getting through in lux.

5   Test elasticity using a force metre to stretch materials – measure the force in Newtons and the stretch in millimetres or centimetres.

6   Examine the speed at which jelly dissolves in relation to surface area depending on whether a cube of jelly is cut into halves, quarters, eighths, etc.

7   Test viscosity of liquids by adding different amounts (one, two or three teaspoons) of wallpaper paste to 200 ml water and then testing the mixtures by dropping a one penny coin into them and counting how long it takes in seconds to fall to the bottom.

All of the above require learners to read numbers from a scale and often to write and interpret numbers. In examples 3 and 4, you could go on to test different pairs of sunglasses and give the materials numerical values, perhaps measuring the distance at which black text on a grey background becomes difficult to read.

Teaching tip

With other characteristics like texture, no unit of measurement is easily available for primary learners. Much could be learnt if learners were asked to invent their own unit of texture or roughness, or better still an index of roughness (note that roughness links in science to friction). For example:

Texture level 1 = smooth

Texture level 2 = some imperfection in the surface

Texture level 3 = some noticeable roughness

Texture level 4 = quite rough

Texture level 5 = very rough, uncomfortable to the touch

This activity would also harness and develops learners' mathematical skills of reasoning and problem solving.

Teaching activities linking mathematics and science

Key Stage 1

Topic: Children's literature

Activity: Materials to help the Three Little Pigs

All sorts of mathematics and science work can develop from a well-known story. The traditional tale of the Three Little Pigs is an example that can be used to initiate tests on different house building materials. Can we build walls and design a test to evaluate their strength? Record how many bricks would be used to build each wall. An alternative is to select and test different materials for the pigs' weather-proof clothing, or the Wolf's shopping bag or warm jacket. At each stage, learners should discuss the physical properties of the materials and why these materials are then considered appropriate for the task at hand. Encourage learners to think logically and reason through their decisions.

NC science objectives

- Ask simple questions and recognise that they can be answered in different ways (Key Stage 1 working scientifically);
- Perform simple tests (Key Stages 1 and 2 working scientifically);
- Distinguish between an object and the material it is made from (Year 1 everyday materials);
- Describe the simple physical properties of a variety of everyday materials (Year 1 everyday materials).

NC mathematics objectives

- Compare, describe and solve practical problems for length and height, and mass and weight (Year 1 measurement);
- Ask and answer questions about totalling and comparing categorical data (Year 1 statistics);

- Solve one-step problems that involve addition and subtraction, using concrete objects and pictorial representations (Year 1 number – addition and subtraction).

Topic: Grouping materials

Activity: Grouping materials

Ask learners to collect a set of everyday materials. An alternative or extension is to identify them in the room or building and make a set of labelled photographs using simple labels. Can they describe the materials using terms such as hard, soft, rough, smooth, cold to touch, warm to touch, prickly, shiny, dull, heavy for size, light for size, see through, not see through, magnetic, non-magnetic, colour? Can they use mathematical language to describe the objects (e.g. the number of sides, edges, vertices and faces)? You might ask them to explain why a material is used for a particular task. Finally, ask them to put the materials into groups. When they have established groups, you might ask them to subdivide the groups. Examining one another's groups and speaking and listening about the groupings will aid all the children's learning. You might introduce a new material and ask them to place it in the correct group.

NC science objectives

- Identify and classify (Key Stage 1 working scientifically);

- Identify and name a variety of common materials, including wood, plastic, glass, metal, water and rock (Year 1 everyday materials);

- Compare and group together a variety of everyday materials on the basis of their simple physical properties (Year 1 everyday materials).

NC mathematics objectives

- Interpret and construct simple pictograms, tally charts, block diagrams and simple tables (Year 2 statistics);

- Identify and describe the properties of 2-D shapes, including the number of sides and line symmetry in a vertical line (Year 2 geometry – properties of shapes).

Key Stage 2

Topic: Rocks

Activity: Rocks suitable for building

Ask learners to observe a selection of rocks, such as granite, sandstone, slate, chalk, limestone and coal. Discuss whether these rocks would be good for building walls, bridges or pavements? Can they say why?

Allow learners to observe the rock surfaces closely with a magnifying glass and record what they see. Can they use their mathematical knowledge of the properties of shape to describe the geometrical features of the rocks? Encourage them to use language such as angle, line of symmetry and parallel. Allow them to scratch the rock with their fingernail, predicting and describing the result. Allow them to scratch the rock with a steel nail, predicting and describing the result. Challenge them to order the rocks from most hard to least hard.

NC science objectives

- Set up simple practical enquiries, comparative and fair tests (Lower Key Stage 2 working scientifically);
- Compare and group together different rocks on the basis of their appearance and physical properties (Year 3 rocks).

NC mathematics objectives

- Identify horizontal and vertical lines and pairs of perpendicular and parallel lines (Year 3 geometry – properties of shapes);
- Interpret and present discrete and continuous data using appropriate graphical methods, including bar charts and time graphs (Year 4 statistics).

Topic: Changing materials

Activity: Turning the heat up

Ask learners to observe solid chocolate, wrapped in cling film and warmed in the hand. Can they measure the temperature of the chocolate before (room temperature) and after (warmed by the hand)? Can they devise and conduct a similar investigation with different chocolate, fudge, butter, margarine and wax?

Use a candle and a small tin tray to allow learners to predict and observe what happens to these materials when heated to a higher temperature. Ask them to talk about the change from solid to liquid. Ask them about other times when they have seen this occur. How long did it take to change shape? Would a bigger/smaller sample change more quickly or more slowly? Ask learners to convert between seconds, minutes and hours. Predict how long it would take if the sample was ten times bigger?

NC science objectives

- Set up simple practical enquiries, comparative and fair tests (Lower Key Stage 2 working scientifically);

- Identify differences, similarities or changes related to simple scientific ideas and processes (Lower Key Stage 2 working scientifically);

- Compare and group materials together, according to whether they are solids, liquids or gases (Year 4 states of matter).

NC mathematics objectives

- Compare the duration of events (Year 3 measurement);

- Solve problems involving converting from hours to minutes, minutes to seconds, years to months and weeks to days (Year 4 measurement).

Topic: Solutions

Activity: Finding the solution

After predicting what will happen, observe exactly what does happen when learners mix a small amount of one material (e.g. water) with another material (e.g. sand, salt, flour, sugar). Ask them to observe and record in words the results.

Ask learners to observe a small piece of jelly dissolving in warm water. Explain that this might look like the jelly melting but that in fact it is dissolving. Repeat this task but time how long the jelly takes to dissolve. Ask learners to devise an investigation to find out what will happen to the speed at which jelly dissolves at different temperatures. You will need to provide thermometers (beware safety), very cold and quite hot water (again, beware safety), beakers, stirrers, timers and perhaps an investigation planning framework. Stress to them that the test must be fair, that they will measure time and temperature and will present the results on a graph.

NC science objectives

- Take measurements, using a range of scientific equipment, with increasing accuracy and precision, taking repeat readings when appropriate (Upper Key Stage 2 working scientifically);

- Understand that some materials will dissolve in liquid to form a solution (Year 6 properties and changes of materials).

NC mathematics objectives

- Enumerate combinations of two variables (Year 6 algebra);

- Solve comparison, sum and difference problems using information presented in a line graph (Year 5 statistics).

Conclusion

Materials is an important part of primary science. You will have seen how this science is all around us in the natural and made world. Because learners can work with materials that are familiar to them, the topic is meaningful. Materials offers many opportunities in science to develop learners' scientific enquiry and mathematical thinking. If you have the measuring equipment, you have the opportunity to test materials and obtain numeric results, thus allowing the presentation and use of data to address questions and conjectures.

Summary of learning

In this chapter, you will have learned:

- that there are many opportunities to conduct investigations;
- about a range of materials and their features;
- that this is a rich area for study of changes to materials;
- that there are numerous opportunities to employ and enrich mathematics and science education within real investigations.

15

Animal Biology

This chapter will ensure that you:

- know about the Animal Kingdom and ways to group animals;

- the importance of variety in the living world and some of the life processes of animals;

- how science and mathematics support one another in this part of biology.

Overview

Learners are generally very interested in animals they encounter and hear about. These include animals in gardens and parks, animals in the wild in the UK and abroad, as well as pets. Animal biology is a very broad subject about which you may have some personal interest and knowledge. To teach about animals you don't need a vast knowledge of all animals. However, a basic understanding of well-known animals in the main groups of the Animal Kingdom (mammals, reptiles, insects, fish, birds and others such as crustaceans, molluscs and amphibians) will help greatly. You may find that some primary aged learners are themselves very knowledgeable about, for example, dogs or horses. The biology of human beings is usually emphasised in primary science, so knowledge of the main external and internal body parts is essential (Figure 15.1).

You will be able to strengthen learning of both mathematics and science by utilising options that require the use of mathematics (e.g. using a heart rate monitor before and after gentle exercise). There will be opportunities to develop mathematical problem solving, reasoning and the science enquiry skills of working

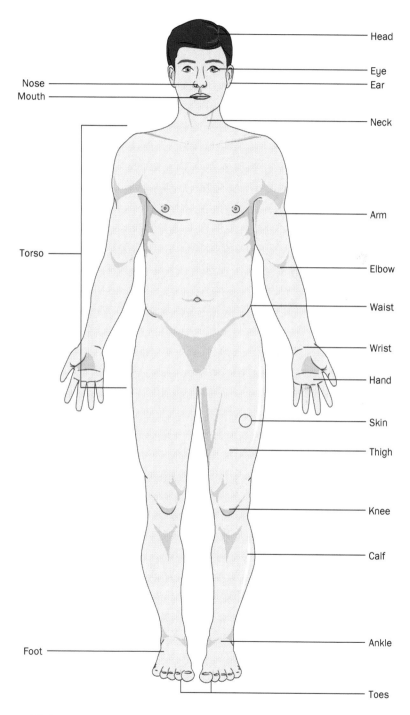

Figure 15.1 Diagrams of human external body parts, internal organs and skeleton

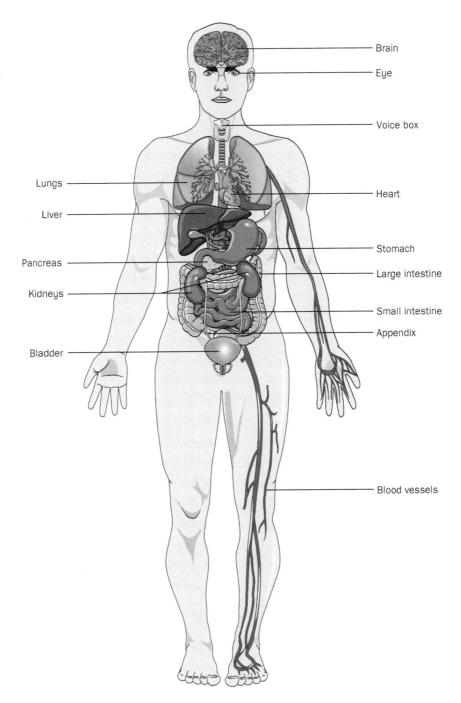

Figure 15.1 Diagrams of human external body parts, internal organs and skeleton

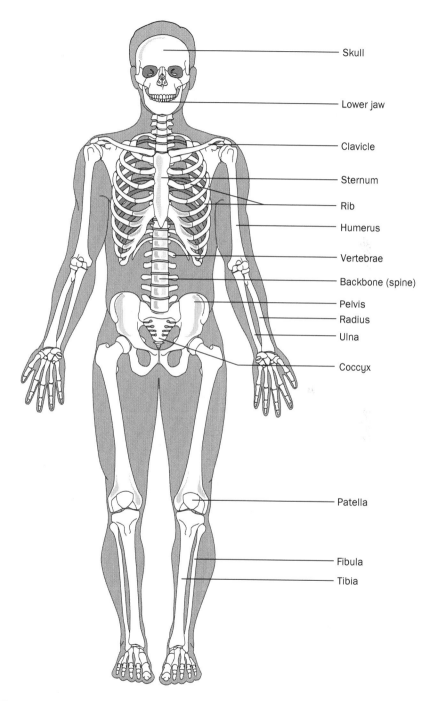

Figure 15.1 Diagrams of human external body parts, internal organs and skeleton

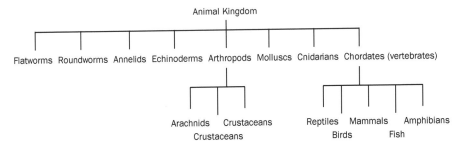

Figure 15.2 A simple version of the Animal Kingdom

scientifically. Grouping and classifying is one important skill of working scientifically that is easy to develop in animal biology (Figure 15.2).

Learners are expected to identify and name common British animals, such as squirrel, field mouse, mole, rat, sparrow, robin, pigeon, cabbage white butterfly, dragon fly, frog, newt, slug, snail and earthworm. You should be able to identify these yourself; however, it is not your job to identify them for learners but to teach them to identify animals themselves by using secondary sources and getting to know the animals. Learners tend to be more familiar with mammals such as mice, sheep, cows and horses. These mammals feature in children's stories, games and songs, which accounts at least partly for this familiarity. Learning to group these animals and to make and use of Carroll diagrams, identification keys, etc. for classification means that both science and mathematics skills are developed.

> **Teaching tip**
> Talk to the learners about the main groups of animals in the Animal Kingdom. Do they know these groups? Can they name and perhaps talk about animals in each group? You might ask groups of learners to research a category each and perhaps create a display, booklet or app about their chosen animal category.

Variation and diversity is an important part of biology and can be introduced through the features of our bodies, starting with those of the learners themselves. Links can be made to mathematics and to physical, social and health education by grouping individuals by gender, hair colour, eye colour, preferences, favourite pastimes and behaviours. It is important to stress similarity as well as difference. We are similar to one another in many ways. Interestingly, as humans we tend to notice and focus on differences rather than similarities.

An important overarching theme is the value of variety in the world and the interdependence of all living things on planet Earth. Strong links can be made here to pattern in mathematics. The study of animals links to learning about the environment and how we can protect our environment.

Animal biology requires us to teach about different life cycles, including those of:

- a mammal – the human life cycle (baby, child, adult, baby);
- a reptile – the life cycle of a lizard (egg, young, adult, egg);
- an amphibian – the life cycle of the frog (egg, tadpole, froglet, frog, egg);
- a fish – the life cycle of salmon (egg, fry, adult fish, egg);
- an insect – the life cycle of a butterfly (egg, caterpillar (lava), chrysalis, butterfly, egg);
- a bird – the life cycle of a blackbird (egg, chick, adult, egg);
- a mollusc – the life cycle of a snail (egg, young snail, adult snail, egg).

For web-based interactive life cycles, go to http://www.topmarks.co.uk/interactive.aspx?cat=64.

Notice that most life cycles begin with eggs. As humans are mammals, the human egg develops inside the mother until birth. As a primary teacher, you are expected to teach about relationships and sex education, and you should consult your school's sex and relationships education policy. In science, we teach about the stages in the human life cycle and how bodies change. We teach that reproduction occurs but not about the mechanics involved; this falls under relationships and sex education, to which health professionals often contribute.

An example of a scientist

Jane Goodall is a renowned scientist and a world expert on the behaviour of chimpanzees (Figure 15.3). She has studied chimpanzees for more than fifty years. Her research is an example to us of working scientifically. Hers were a series of observational studies over time in the Tanzanian Gombe Stream National Park. Although her methods were far from orthodox, she used mathematics to record the chronology of observations and to film, time and classify different individuals and behaviours. She observed forms of tool use, tool making and aggression in chimpanzees which had never been seen before and which changed thinking about animal behaviour and its significance for scientists interested in early man and current human behaviour. Find out more at www.janegoodall.co.uk. (There is an activity about chimpanzee DNA in Chapter 5: Pattern.)

Figure 15.3 Pencil sketch of Jane Goodall (1934–)

Connecting mathematics and science: animal biology

Primary teachers have a great deal to choose from when looking at animal life but need to be very selective if they are to progress learners' science knowledge and the ability to work scientifically. If you feel the Programme of Study (DfE, 2013) limits your scope, focus on 'working scientifically' and consider objectives from other age groups and links to other subjects. Mathematics can help considerably here, such as dealing with numbers when planning a calorie-controlled diet. Other examples include:

- researching animal statistics (size, mass, etc.) through secondary research;
- classifying animals;
- creating a database of animals;
- measuring the movements of wood lice in a tray;
- estimating the size and weight of birds observed, checking learners' estimates against a database.

Primary learners are usually very interested in the human body, such as the human heart and pulse rate. The data shown in Figure 15.4 were recorded by primary learners, who were able to explain the difference in pulse rate and strength in terms of the physical activity of the individuals.

A real-life example with mathematics and science

Among other things, the Royal Society for the Protection of Birds (RSPB) seeks to protect bird species in danger. They count and monitor individual animals, breeding

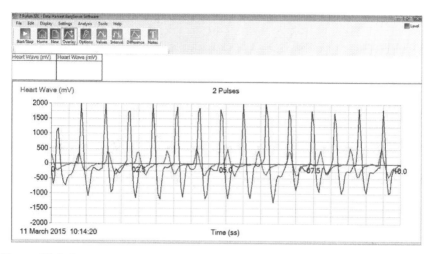

Figure 15.4 Data downloaded from a data logger showing the pulses of two learners
Reproduced with permission from Data Harvest Group (http://www.data-harvest.
co.uk/catalogue/science/primary/datalogging/primary-vu-data-logger/2300PK)

Teaching tip

Show learners how to take their pulse for fifteen seconds and how, by
multiplying by four, they can calculate their pulse over one minute. Ask
learners to investigate one or more of the following:

- What is my resting pulse rate?
- Does pulse rate change as people get older?
- What is my pulse rate after gentle exercise?
- Following exercise, how long does it take for my pulse rate to return
  to the resting rate?

---

pairs and clutch sizes. Databases are constructed following the monitoring of bird
numbers year on year so that any fall in numbers can be identified and, if necessary, action considered. Like other organisations, the RSPB runs an annual public involvement survey in which children can participate. This is real science using
mathematics to produce useful datasets. The RSPB annual bird watch scheme
allows the public to record bird species observed in a garden or locality. They also
run a version for schools called the Big Schools Birdwatch (Table 15.1). Find more
information at:

https://www.rspb.org.uk/birdwatch/

Table 15.1 Dataset from the RSPB's Birdwatch (2015)

Species	Mean	Rank	Percent gardens	Percent change since 2014
House sparrow	4.254	1	64.58	12.3
Starling	2.957	2	43.92	24.5
Blackbird	2.753	3	91.63	26.9
Blue tit	2.737	4	81.55	11.4
Woodpigeon	2.018	5	70.29	19.8
Chaffinch	1.445	6	42.39	–3.5
Robin	1.443	7	86.53	31.4
Great tit	1.399	8	56.72	11.9
Goldfinch	1.300	9	28.38	–8.8
Collared dove	1.205	10	47.96	3.6
Magpie	1.146	11	52.65	24.8
Dunnock	0.905	12	45.72	11.3
Long tailed tit	0.809	13	22.10	5.3
Feral pigeon	0.761	14	19.57	22.8
Carrion crow	0.756	15	27.68	54.6
Jackdaw	0.713	16	20.22	29.6
Coal tit	0.565	17	29.89	5.5
Greenfinch	0.461	18	18.02	–17.0
Wren	0.348	19	28.94	95.4
Common gull	0.337	20	7.35	515.5

Other public involvement surveys include those on insects and invertebrates at:

http://www.bbc.co.uk/breathingplaces/ladybird-survey/

http://www.bigbutterflycount.org

http://www.opalexplorenature.org/SpeciesQuestBugs

Key teaching points for animal biology

Animals provide a context about which learners will have a range of questions. Learners will accept that there is a lot to find out and will be very enthusiastic 'sponges' for knowledge about animals, including facts and data. They will be interested in mathematical facts about animals such as size, location, range, speed, longevity and brood size. Learners can be asked to describe animals in all sorts of ways that include the use of mathematics. Access to animals can add to this work in science and mathematics. Advice should be followed in *Be Safe!* (ASE, 2014).

Teaching tip

You might ask learners to calculate the growth of a population of, say, 20 rabbits, given a litter size of six kittens (baby rabbits) and two litters a year. Increase the challenge by asking learners to account for a mortality rate of, say, one-fifth of the population per year.

Teaching activities linking mathematics to science

Key Stage 1

Topic: Animals in the local area

Activity: Evidence of animals

Take learners for a walk around the school site or further afield. Before doing so, ask them what they think they may see in terms of animal life. Will they see animals? Will they see evidence of animals – a chewed stick, a nest? Explain that in order to see animals they need to be quiet, as animals will hear them and want to hide.

Return to the classroom and ask them to think in pairs about ways that they could record the animals they observed on the walk. They might suggest drawings, writing and photographs. Ask learners to consider producing a booklet or data file on animal life on the site. The class could then form teams to observe and record different aspects of animal life involving bird life, earthworms, mammals, and so on. Explain that whenever possible, they should use mathematics. Show learners how their mathematical skills support their science enquiry by reading numbers, collecting and sorting data, and using their problem-solving skills. A visit to a local nature reserve would be of great benefit.

If the class show a real interest, pursue the science and mathematics more deeply, for example:

- Does this animal hibernate?
- Does the length of the day in different seasons affect the animal?
- What is the clutch/brood size? If all the babies lived, what would the population growth look like after five or ten generations?
- How far does the animal roam in a day? Week? Year?

NC science objectives

- Observe closely, using simple equipment (Key Stage 1 working scientifically);
- Identify and classify (Key Stage 1 working scientifically);
- Identify and name a variety of common animals, including fish, amphibians, reptiles, birds and mammals (Year 1 animals, including humans).

NC mathematics objectives

- Count to and across 100, forwards and backwards, beginning with 0 or 1, or from any given number (Year 1 number – number and place value);
- Ask and answer simple questions by counting the number of objects in each category and sorting categories by quantity (Year 2 statistics).

Topic: Keeping fit and healthy

Activity: Designing an exercise plan

After warning learners that we should not exercise too vigorously, ask them to talk about and then share different forms of exercise. Collate a set of options together, then ask them in pairs or groups of three to gently try them out. Model how an exercise plan might look, for example, ten star jumps, rest, five sit-ups, and so on. Ask small groups to devise a gentle plan of exercise for ten minutes. Groups might then supervise one another as they each carry out the plan of another group.

Ask learners to talk about the plan and ask why exercise is important, for example, it strengthens muscles, strengthens your heart, makes you feel good, its good for your circulation, digestion, nerves, helps control weight, etc.

Challenge learners to predict and take their pulse rate before and after the exercises and record the results.

NC science objectives

- Making systematic and careful observations and, where appropriate, taking accurate measurements using standard units, using a range of equipment, including thermometers and data loggers (Lower Key Stage 2 working scientifically);

- Describe the importance for humans of exercise, eating the right amounts of different types of food and hygiene (Year 2 animals, including humans).

NC mathematics objectives

- Read and write numbers to at least 100 in numerals and in words (Year 2 number – number and place value);

- Ask and answer questions about totalling and comparing categoric data (Year 2 statistics).

Key Stage 2

Topic: Animals in the wild

Activity: Predator and prey

Model a simple game based on rabbits and foxes in a wood. Explain that there are one hundred rabbits in the wood and they have five babies a month. Together with learners, construct a graph of the rabbit population over the coming months.

Now explain that there are two foxes who eat five rabbits each a week and have two cubs each (you can vary these parameters). Ask learners to add these data to the graph using a different coloured line. Can they talk about the affect this has on the rabbit population? What do they think would happen in the future? Can they test a conjecture? Can a population of one hundred foxes live alongside a population of one hundred rabbits?

You could challenge learners further by accessing the models at the following websites:

http://www.shodor.org/interactivate/activities/RabbitsAndWolves/

http://www.abpischools.org.uk/page/modules/population_growth/activity.cfm?coSiteNavigation_allTopic=1

Ask learners about different starting conditions and what they see happening. Can they reason and explain why after a population increase, there is a reduction in the following generation?

NC science objectives

- Use results to draw simple conclusions, make predictions of new values, suggest improvements and raise further questions (Lower Key Stage 2 working scientifically);
- Construct and interpret a variety of food chains, identifying producers, predators and prey (Year 4 animals, including humans).

NC mathematics objectives

- Identify, represent and estimate numbers using different representations (Year 4 number – number and place value);
- Interpret and present discrete and continuous data using appropriate graphical methods, including bar charts and time graphs (Year 4 statistics).

Topic: How do animals move?

Activity: Snail trail

Introduce learners to live snails and stress the need for care, and personal hygiene once snails are handled. Stress also the need to pick them up very gently by the shell and that the body and eyes of the snail are very delicate. Allow learners to observe snails, ideally in white plastic trays with magnifying glasses if possible. Can they describe the shell and skin of the snail? Can they estimate length, width and mass of the snail? Measuring snail length can be difficult, as they rarely stay still. Learners are usually intrigued by snails' sensitive eye stalks and eyes. With care and a magnifying glass they can observe the snail's mouth. In order to observe the snail's foot operating, place the snail carefully on transparent plastic and slowly turn it upside down – learners can then observe the waves of muscular action on the foot that propel the snail. Place this sheet on squared paper to measure the snail's length and distance travelled in thirty seconds or one minute. If possible you might use a visualiser or computer microscope to provide magnified images of the snail's body, movement and eating behaviour.

Once learners have measured distance travelled in thirty seconds or one minute, ask them to calculate the distances travelled over five minutes, ten minutes, an hour, a day, etc. Consider the need for repeat readings. Ask learners to measure the distance travelled by three snails so that they can calculate the mean, mode and median. Can they look at a local map and its scale to see where the snail might reach if it travelled in a straight line? Ask learners to estimate a snail's journey over the summer months. Remember that snails travel in search of food, so they will travel up and down and across one plant for many minutes and so may not travel far at all in a straight line.

NC science objectives

- Take measurements, using a range of scientific equipment, with increasing accuracy and precision, taking repeat readings where necessary (Upper Key Stage 2 working scientifically);

- Describe how living things are classified into broad groups according to common observable characteristics and based on similarities and differences, including micro-organisms, plants and animals (Year 6 living things and their habitats).

NC mathematics objectives

- Use, read, write and convert between standard units, converting measurements of length, mass, volume and time from a smaller unit of measure to a larger unit, and vice versa, using decimal notation up to three decimal places (Year 6 measurement);

- Calculate and interpret the mean as an average (Year 6 statistics).

Conclusion

Human biology is an exciting topic for learners. They will be interested to learn about animals and their lives as well as about their own bodies and about other people. This interest and the numerous examples of number, data, proportionality, geometry and problem solving mean that science links strongly with mathematics. There are more examples throughout the book, for example in Chapter 6 on Measurement where an activity asks, 'are you a square or rectangle?' Learners will begin to appreciate that behind the seemingly straightforward and familiar world of animals lies a great deal of complexity. Much of this can be described in numbers and allows us to understand some of what we see, for example, linking our pulse rate to exercise.

Summary of learning

In this chapter, you will have learned:

- about aspects of animal life, including human life processes;
- about the value of studying human biology and making links to PSHE;
- about several opportunities for the enrichment and development of both mathematics and science;
- appreciated the value of working quantitatively where possible;
- about the need to respect animal life.

16

Plant Biology

This chapter will ensure that you:

- learn about the potential for the study of plants in science to link to the learning of important ideas in mathematics, including properties of shape, time, probability, grouping and classification;

- that the plant world is highly diverse, presenting an awesome array of wonders that will stimulate curiosity and the posing of questions by learners.

Overview

Learners' familiarity with plants varies but may be rather limited, as you will discover when you ask learners to list or talk about plants they can name, or better still, ones they can talk about. This would probably work best on a walk around the school site or local area. Remind them that the group we call plants includes trees.

You may need to develop your knowledge of the Plant Kingdom (Figure 16.1), including that organisms such as fungi are not plants. You are expected to teach children to identify a number of common British plants, including buttercup, daisy, ash tree, poppy, nettle and dock. You might find that field guides to wild flowers (e.g. Phillips, 1977) are often organised around the colour of the plant flower. Can your class describe and group plants they find? Find out more at http://www.naturespot.org.uk/taxonomy/term/19596.

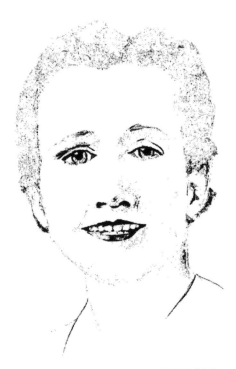

Figure 16.1 Pencil sketch of Rachel Carson (1907–1964)

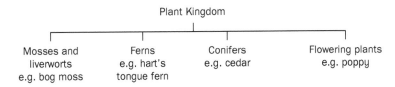

Figure 16.2 A simple version of the Plant Kingdom

An example of a scientist

Rachel Carson was a marine biologist and environmental campaigner (Figure 16.2). She wrote a number of books about the sea and environmentalism, including her seminal work Silent Spring (1962), which brought her and her ideas about the environment to the attention of millions of people around the world.

Rachel campaigned against the use of pesticides, citing data on the decline of, for example, song birds in agricultural areas. She put mathematics to very good use in highlighting patterns, such as those showing declines in animal populations. Find out more at http://www.environmentandsociety.org/exhibitions/silent-spring/overview.

Figure 16.3 Spirals evident in a flower

Connecting mathematics and science: plant biology

Pattern can be observed in the plant world, including the cycles of growth during the year and the life cycles of plants. The arrangements of leaves and other plant parts reveal patterns. Plant growth itself can be measured and tabulated over days and weeks to reveal patterns in the way some plants grow. Questions can be posed and curiosity encouraged. Comparisons can be made between different growing conditions, including varying the intensity of light, the direction of light and the type of soil. Learners can produce growth charts and graphs making simple comparisons and designing fair tests.

As mentioned in Chapter 5, the Fibonacci sequence can be observed in plants. It is often present in the number of petals in flowers (3, 5, 8, 13, 21) and spirals in the inflorescence (21 and 34, 34 and 55, 55 and 89, etc.) (Figure 16.3). It can also be observed in the leaves on a palm, the flowers on a daisy and the scales of a cone. There is no doubt that we find many aspects of the plant world interesting and beautiful and these patterns are one of the features. Find out more at http://www.popmath.org.uk/rpamaths/rpampages/sunflower.html.

Other mathematical connections are explored through: numbers and arrangements of petals and leaves; grouping and classifying plants; recording the growth of seedlings and plants; keeping a plant growth diary; calculating the height, girth and canopy size of trees; mean seedling height.

A real-life example with mathematics and science

Involving a class in growing vegetables and flowers from seed for a school allotment demands the skills of working mathematically and scientifically. Subject knowledge, understanding and skills from both mathematics and science will be employed through logical planning, an awareness of the calendar – the seasons, days and weeks – successional sowing, depth, temperature, planting distances, cycles, geometry and shape.

The science involved includes the seasons, plant growth, life processes, plant parts, cycles and human nutrition. From here it is a small step to personal, social and health education and design and technology for making food. How many children handle, prepare and eat food they have grown? Always warn children that we eat safe plants and the safe parts of plants, but that many plants are or have parts that are poisonous.

If children have parents who encourage them to take an interest in plants and plant growth, they may have had rich experiences on walks, when planting bulbs and even perhaps on allotments. Some schools will be involved with EnCams Eco Schools (http://www.eco-schools.org.uk) and schemes run by organisations such as the Woodland Trust (https://www.woodlandtrust.org.uk). From time to time there will be opportunities to carry out and contribute to national surveys, such as that on biodiversity.

Key teaching points for plant biology

Growing plants from seed and bulbs is an essential experience that ought to challenge any age group. Begin with straightforward observation and increasingly accurate description. Part of this is measurement of stems, flowers, leaves, roots, etc. Learners can quickly move to simple, comparative and fair tests to find out about different plants and different growing conditions. It is worth keeping in mind that all plants take time to grow and react to their environment, so investigations may be spread over many days.

These experiences will expose learners to the wonders of the Plant Kingdom and stimulate what may become a life-long interest. Because some investigations will take a week or two to complete, you will need to plan your lesson time to include setting up the investigation, caring for and monitoring the plants daily, and completing the investigation. You should also think about the time of year. Bean and cress seeds will germinate indoors throughout the year but generally seeds do better in the spring and warmer months. Don't assume that learners will have much experience of plants. They may have little respect for plants and might routinely damage plants outside the school day. Learners need to be made aware of the value of plants to humans for food and other uses (e.g. cotton for clothing and the oxygen we breathe). Be aware that plant material can be toxic and some children may react to pollen. If in doubt, consult the ASE booklet *Be Safe!* (ASE, 2014).

Teaching activities linking mathematics to science

Key Stage 1

Topic: How do plants grow?

Activity: Growing plants

Young children are usually very interested in plants and will more often than not have observed a range of plants in homes, gardens and parks. They will recognise plants or parts of plants they eat, though they may not see the link between the flowering plant on the windowsill and a potato. They may know that some plants and their seeds are poisonous. Science and mathematics provide great opportunities for learners to grow plants of different kinds and to observe the shape, colours and textures of the leaves, to group and classify, and to match flowers to plants and plants to habitats where they are found.

Young learners need to learn about the conditions needed for plant growth. At this stage, the sowing of seeds followed by a study over time of their germination and growth is a great opportunity for learners to develop an interest in and a love of the natural world. It is also a fantastic context for the learning and development of science and mathematics skills (e.g. measurement).

NC science objectives

- Ask simple questions and recognise that they can be answered in different ways (Key Stage 1 working scientifically);
- Observe closely using simple equipment (Key Stage 1 working scientifically);
- Gather and record data to help in answering questions (Key Stage 1 working scientifically);
- Observe and describe how seeds and bulbs grow into mature plants (Year 2 plants);
- Find out and describe how plants need water, light and a suitable temperature to grow and stay healthy (Year 2 plants).

NC mathematics objectives

- Describe position, direction and movement including whole, half, quarter, and three-quarter turns (Year 1 geometry – position and direction);

- Compare and order lengths, mass, volume/capacity and record the results using >, < and = (Year 2 measurement);
- Compare and sequence intervals of time (Year 2 measurement);
- Interpret and construct simple pictograms, tally charts, block diagrams and simple tables (Year 2 statistics);
- Ask and answer questions about totalling and comparing categoric data (Year 2 statistics).

Topic: Are all plants the same?

Activity: Observing the parts of plants

In both mathematics and science, observation is a key skill. In both subjects, it is important to be able to use the language of geometry. Asking learners to observe and describe a variety of plants can help develop these skills. Warn learners that plants that are not sold to be eaten may be poisonous. A selection of potted plants would make a great basis for a lesson that challenges learners to describe the plants in as much detail as possible (e.g. leaf size, shape, texture, colour, stem colour, appearance, arrangement of leaves on the plant). If possible, allow the learners to observe the roots for a while. If you are unable to access potted plants, you could dig up a selection of weeds (wild flowers) from a cultivated garden. Tell learners that picking or damaging plants in the wild is against the law. Ask learners to create a poster or web page for each plant. If they can't find its name, can they name it themselves?

NC science objectives

- Observe closely, using simple equipment (Key Stage 1 working scientifically);
- Identify and describe the basic structure of a variety of common flowering plants (Year 1 plants).

NC mathematics objectives

- Recognise and name common 2-D shapes (e.g. rectangles including squares) and 3-D shapes (e.g. cuboids including cubes; pyramids and spheres) (Year 1 geometry – properties of shapes).

Key Stage 2

Topic: The tallest plants

Activity: The tallest living thing in school!

Young children will be interested in the giants of the plant world, including the Giant Redwoods in California, some of which are over 370 feet (115 metres) tall. Find out more about measuring the height of these tall trees at http://www.monumentaltrees.com/en/trees/coastredwood/video/.
Challenge the children to research tall garden plants they can grow from seed. These will include varieties of sunflower, a plant that will grow taller than every child in a primary school within a few weeks. It might even dwarf the adults! Challenge learners to research the growing conditions required, the time of sowing and care for best results. Although these plants require feeding, ensure learners understand that plants get their energy from sunlight. Ask them to pose a question, plan and carry out an investigation of the growth of these tall plants.

NC science objectives

- Set up simple practical enquiries, comparative and fair tests (Lower Key Stage 2 working scientifically);
- Record findings using simple scientific language, drawings, labelled diagrams, keys, bar charts and tables (Lower Key Stage 2 working scientifically);
- Identify and describe the functions of different parts of flowering plants: roots, stem/trunk, leaves and flowers (Year 3 plants);
- Explore the requirements of plants for life and growth (air, light, water, nutrients from soil, and room to grow) and how they vary from plant to plant (Year 3 plants).

NC mathematics objectives

- Read and write numbers to at least one hundred in numerals and words (Year 3 number – number and place value);
- Choose and use appropriate standard units to estimate and measure length/height in any direction (m/cm); mass (kg/g); temperature (°C), and capacity (l/ml) to the nearest appropriate unit, using rulers, scales, thermometers and measuring vessels (Year 3 measurement);
- Compare and sequence intervals of time (Year 3 measurement);
- Interpret and construct simple pictograms, tally charts, block diagrams and simple tables (Year 3 statistics).

Topic: Conditions for plant growth

Activity: Exploring plant growth

Challenge a class to explore all aspects of plant growth listed from the National Curriculum below. Can groups of learners design, plan and carry out investigations of the needs of plants in various conditions? Can they design comparative tests? Fair tests? The two most challenging tests involve air and room to grow. There is no particularly effective test in the primary school for the effect of air versus no air; a vacuum is beyond the capability of a primary teacher to engineer! However, you could wrap the stem and leaves of a potted plant in a large transparent plastic bag (note the safety aspect here). Learners can observe the moisture that will appear in the bag. Comparisons might be made to another plant but conclusions regarding growth will be very difficult to make.

It will be easier to compare growth in seedlings. For example, compare the growth of thirty seeds sown apart with that of thirty seeds sown in a confined space. Measurement will present a challenge but it is possible that a difference will be seen.

NC science objectives

- Make systematic and careful observations and, where appropriate, take accurate measurements using standard units, using a range of equipment, including thermometers and data loggers (Lower Key Stage 2 working scientifically);

- Explore the requirements of plants for life and growth (air, light, water, nutrients from soil, and room to grow) and how they vary from plant to plant. (Year 3 plants).

NC mathematics objectives

- Compare and order numbers up to 1000 (Year 3 number – number and place value);

- Solve problems that involve fractions (Year 3 fractions);

- Interpret and present data using bar charts, pictograms and tables (Year 3 statistics).

Topic: Evolution

Activity: Eaten and beaten?

The characteristic colour or pattern on a seed can influence its survival. This might affect whether it will grow to adulthood and therefore whether its genes are passed on. This activity shows learners that some seeds are better camouflaged and so will be less likely to be eaten and more likely to pass on their genes.

Prepare five or so types of large seed (e.g. green lentil, brown broad bean, white bean) ensuring that you have one hundred of each; fifty would be okay, as children can double each result to get a percentage. Scatter the seeds over a measured one-metre square of grass. Then give a group thirty seconds to retrieve as many seeds as possible. After collecting and counting these seeds, simple subtraction calculations will tell the learners how many of each seed type were not collected and used in a repeat test by another group. (Learners ought then to collect the seeds left on the ground to confirm numbers and then make use of the seeds in a growth experiment or in pots for a later crop of vegetables.) The data should reveal a difference in numbers based on how well camouflaged the seeds are. You might then lead a very useful discussion as to the effect of this camouflage on the numbers of young plants for the following generations (Figure 16.4). The learners may come to appreciate how a feature such as camouflage could reduce the numbers of plants and therefore the extent to which a particular plant will be successful. Extend this discussion by asking what would happen if other animals came to the area, thus increasing the numbers of seeds eaten?

NC science objectives

- Identify scientific evidence that has been used to support or refute ideas or arguments (Upper Key Stage 2 working scientifically);

- Identify how animals and plants are adapted to suit their environment in different ways and that adaptation may lead to evolution (Year 5 evolution and inheritance).

NC mathematics objectives

- Use rounding to check answers to calculations and determine, in the context of a problem, levels of accuracy (Year 5 number – addition and subtraction);

- Recognise the percent symbol (%) and understand that percent relates to 'number of parts per hundred', and write percentages as a fraction with the denominator 100 and as a decimal (Year 5 number – fractions, including decimals and percentages).

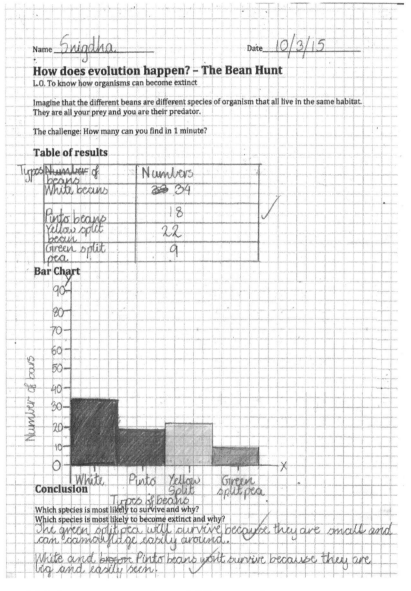

Figure 16.4 Testing the camouflage of different seeds

Conclusion

The life processes of plants offer primary learners the opportunity to use mathematics in science when investigating real questions. Humans have studied plants for many generations, and we have learnt to care for them and to get the best out of them. Advances in science mean that plants will contribute more and more in terms of foods, medicines and other products. Our understanding of and interactions with plants rely on science and mathematics, so the combination of the two here is very natural.

Summary of learning

In this chapter, you will have learned:

- about the variety of the Plant Kingdom, thus promoting curiosity;
- about the potential of plants as a context for learning about science and mathematics;
- about some of the associated challenges using growing plants in the classroom;
- that there are safety issues related to this topic.

Bibliography

Abrahams, I. and Millar, R. (2008) Does practical work really work? A study of the effectiveness of practical work as a teaching and learning method in school science, *International Journal of School Science Education*, 30 (14): 1945–69.

Advisory Committee on Mathematics Education (ACME) (2011) *Mathematical Needs*. London: ACME.

Ahmed, A. (1987) *Better Mathematics: A Curriculum Development Study*. London: HMSO.

Alexander, R. (2010) *Children, Their World, Their Education: Final Report and Recommendations of the Cambridge Primary Review*. London: Routledge.

Allen, M. (2010) *Misconceptions in Primary Science*. Maidenhead: Open University Press.

Askew, A., Brown, M., Rhodes, V., Wiliam, D. and Johnson, D. (1997) *Effective Teachers of Numeracy*. London: King's College.

Association of Science Education (ASE) (1990) *The Earth in Space*. Hatfield: ASE.

Association of Science Education (ASE) (2014) *Be Safe!* (4th edn.). Hatfield: ASE.

Barnes, J. (2011) *Cross-Curricular Learning 3–14* (2nd edn.). London: Sage.

Boaler, J. (2009) *The Elephant in the Classroom: Helping Children to Love Maths*. London: Souvenir Press.

Borthwick, A. (2011) Children's perceptions of, and attitudes towards, their mathematics lessons, in E. Smith (ed.) *Proceedings of the British Society for Research into Learning Mathematics*, 31 (1), 37–42.

Borthwick, A. and Harcourt-Heath, M. (2015) Calculating: how have Year 5 children's strategies changed over time? *Proceedings of the British Society for Research into Learning Mathematics*, 34 (3): 1–6.

Brodie, M. and Fuller, N. (2012) Pattern seeking, *Primary Science*, 124: 5–7.

Browne, E. (2006) *Handa's Surprise*. London: Walker Books.

Burton, L. (1994) *Children Learning Mathematics: Patterns and Relationships*. Hemel Hempstead: Prentice-Hall/IBD.

Carle, E. (2010) *The Bad-Tempered Ladybird*. London: Puffin Books.

Carroll, L. (2001) *Alice's Adventures in Wonderland*. London: Walker Books.

Carroll, L. (2008) *Alice Through the Looking Glass*. London: Walker Books.

Carson, R. (1962) *Silent Spring*. London: Penguin Books.

Cockroft, W.H. (1982) *Mathematics Counts*. London: The Stationery Office.

Cross, A. (2012) *ITT Teach! Primary Science App for Smartphones and Tablets* [http://www.cc-apps.co.uk/page/109/Science.htm].

Cross, A. and Board, J. (2015) Playground science, *Primary Science*, 136: 24–6.

Cross, A. and Bowden, A. (2014) *Essential Primary Science* (2nd edn.). Maidenhead: Open University Press.

Deboys, M. and Pitt, E. (1988) *Lines of Development in Primary Mathematics* (3rd edn.). Belfast: Blackstaff Press.

Department for Education (DfE) (2013) *The National Curriculum in England: Key Stages 1 and 2 Framework Document*. London: DfE [http://dera.ioe.ac.uk/18300/1/PRIMARY_national_curriculum.pdf].

Department for Education and Employment (DfEE) (1999) *The National Numeracy Curriculum: Handbook for Primary Teachers in England, Key Stages 1 and 2*. London: DfEE.

Department of Education and Science (DES) (1979) *Mathematics 5–11: A Handbook of Suggestions*. Matters for Discussion 9. London: HMSO [http://www.educationengland.org.uk/documents/hmi-discussion/maths-primary.html].

Feasey, R. and Gallear, B. (2000) *Primary Science and Numeracy*. Hafield: ASE.

Freedman, C. (2007) *Aliens Love Underpants*. London: Simon & Schuster.

Fromental, J.-L. (2006) *365 Penguins*. New York: Abrams Books.

Goldsworthy, A. and Feasey, R. (1997) *Making Sense of Primary Science Investigations*. Hatfield: ASE.

Goldsworthy, A., Watson, R. and Wood-Robinson, V. (1999) *Getting to Grips With Graphs*. Hatfield: ASE.

Goldsworthy, A., Watson, R. and Wood Robinson, V. (2000) *Developing Understanding in Scientific Enquiry*. Hatfield: ASE.

Hansen, A. (ed.) (2014) *Children's Errors in Mathematics* (3rd edn.). London: Learning Matters.

Hardy, G. H. (1940) *A Mathematician's Apology*. Cambridge: Cambridge University Press.

Harlen, W. (1999) *Effective Teaching of Science: A Review of Research*. Edinburgh: Scottish Council for Research in Education.

Harlen, W. (2010) Teaching primary science: how research helps, *Primary Science*, 114: 5–8.

Hattie, J. (2009) *Visible Learning*. Abingdon: Routledge.

Haylock, D. (2010) *Mathematics Explained for Primary Teachers*. London: Sage.

Haylock, D. and Cockburn, A. (2008) *Understanding Mathematics for Young Children: A Guide for Foundation Stage and Lower Primary Teachers*. London: Sage.

Haynes, J. (2002) *Children as Philosophers*. London: Routledge.

Heath, T.L. (2014) *The Thirteen Books of Euclid's Elements, Vol. 1: Introduction and Books I, II*. Cambridge: Cambridge University Press.

Hendry, S. (2013) Mathematics enhancing science, in L. Kelly and D. Stead (eds.) *Enhancing Primary Science: Developing Effective Cross-Curricular Links*. Maidenhead: Open University Press.

Hilligan, B. (2013) Giving children ownership of their science investigations, *Primary Science*, 128: 5–8.

Hiscock, N. (2012) Making links between maths and science, *Primary Science*, 124: 11–13.

Hoath, L. (2015) Breathing or respiration? *Primary Science*, 137: 12–13.

Hodson, D. (1993) Re-thinking old ways: towards a more critical approach to practical work in school science, *School Science Review*, 73: 65–78.

Hofstein, A. and Lunetta, V. (2004) The laboratory in science education: foundations for the twenty-first century, *Science Education*, 88 (1): 28–54.

Hughes, T. (2005a) *The Iron Man*. London: Faber & Faber.

Hughes, T. (2005b) *The Iron Woman*. London: Faber & Faber.

Johnston-Wilder, S. and Mason, J. (eds.) (2005) *Developing Thinking in Geometry*. London: Paul Chapman.

Jones, L. (2003) The problem with problem solving, in I. Thompson (ed.) *Enhancing Primary Mathematics Teaching*. Maidenhead: Open University Press.

Kipling. R. (1902) *Just So Stories*. London: Macmillan.

Lewis, L. (2001) *Barnaby Bear Goes to Dublin*. London: Geographical Association.

Lovell, J. and Kluger, J. (1994) *Lost Moon: The Perilous Voyage of Apollo 13*. New York: Houghton Miffin.

Lynn, S. (2006) Working like real scientists, *Primary Science*, 94: 4–7.

Milne, A.A. (1926) *Winnie the Pooh*. New York: Dutton.

Moeed, A. (2013) Science investigation that best supports student learning: teachers understanding of science investigation, *International Journal of Environmental and Science Education*, 8: 537–59.

Moomaw, S. (2013) *Teaching STEM in the Early Years*. St. Paul, MN: Redleaf Press.

Naik, M. (2013) Mathematics, in R. Jones and D. Wyse, D. (eds.) *Creativity in the Primary Curriculum* (2nd edn.). London: David Fulton.

Nunes, T., Bryant, P., Sylva, K. and Barros, R. (2009) *Development of Maths Capabilities and Confidence in Primary School*. London: DCSF.

Ofsted (2008) *Mathematics: Understanding the Score*. London: Ofsted.

Ofsted (2010) *Learning: Creative Approaches that Raise Standards*. Manchester: Ofsted.

Ofsted (2011) *Successful Science*. London: Ofsted.

Ofsted (2013) *Maintaining Curiosity*. London: Ofsted.

Osborne, J., Black, P., Smith, M. and Meadows, J. (1991) *SPACE Report: Electricity*. Liverpool: Liverpool University Press [http://www.nuffieldfoundation.org/primary-science-and-space/electricity].

Peirce, B. (1870) *Linear Associative Algebra: A Memoir Read before the National Academy of Sciences in Washington, DC*. Original lithographed limited edition. Washington, DC.

Pennant, J., Woodham, L. and Bagnall, B. (2014) *Reasoning: Identifying Opportunities*. Cambridge: NRICH [www.nrich.maths.org/10990; accessed July 2015].

Phillips, R. (1977) *Wild Flowers of Britain*. London: Pan Field Guides.

Polya, G. (1945) *How to Solve it*. Princeton, NJ: Princeton University Press.

Rose, J. (2009) *Independent Review of the Primary Curriculum: Final Report*. Nottingham: DCSF.

Ross, T. (2003) *Centipede's 100 Shoes*. London: Anderson Press.

Rowling, J.K. (1997) *Harry Potter and the Philosopher's Stone*. London: Bloomsbury.

Russell, S.J. (2000) Developing computational fluency with whole numbers in the elementary grades, in B.J. Ferrucci and K.M. Heid (eds.) Millennium Focus Issue: Perspectives on Principles and Standards, *New England Maths Journal*, XXXII (2): 40–54.

Sawyer, W.W. (1955) *A Prelude to Mathematics*. London: Penguin.

Schoenfeld, A.H. (1994) *Mathematical Thinking and Problem Solving*. Oxford: Routledge.

Seeley, C. (2012) Astromaths explored!, *Primary Science*, 124: 27cien

Serin, G. (2014) Learning about the weather through a STEM approach, *Primary Science*, 132: 28–30.

Shields, T. (2012) Real life maths and science, *Primary Science*, 124: 24–6.

Shoshan, B. (2004) *Memory Bottles*. London: Meadowside Children's Books.

Skemp, R. (1976) Relational understanding and instrumental understanding, *Mathematics Teaching*, 77: 20–6.

Spendlove, D. and Cross, A. (2013) Design and technology, in R. Jones and D. Wyse, D. (eds.) *Creativity in the Primary Curriculum* (2nd edn.). London: David Fulton.

The Royal Society (2014, June) *Vision for Science and Mathematics Education*. London: The Royal Society [https://royalsociety.org/~/media/education/policy/vision/reports/vision-full-report-20140625.pdf].

Thompson, I., Treffers, A. and Beishuizen, M. (1999) *Issues in Teaching Numeracy in Primary Schools*. Buckingham: Open University Press.

Thompson, I. and Bramald, R. (2002) *An Investigation of the Relationship between Young Childrenreports/vision-full-report-20140625.pdf].rds in Education.Developing Effective Cross-C*. Newcastle: University of Newcastle, Department of Education.

Treahy, I. (2012) *Jack and the Beanstalk*. London: Penguin Books.

Turner, J. (2012) It's not fair!, *Primary Science*, 121: 30–3.

Turner, J., Keogh, B., Naylor, S. and Lawrence, L. (2011) *It's Not Fair – Or is it?* Sandbach: Millgate House/Hatfield: ASE.

Van Hiele, P. (1999) Developing geometric thinking through activities that begin with play, *Teaching Children Mathematics*, 5: 310–16.Wallace. B., Cave, D. and Berry, A. (2008) *Teaching Problem-Solving and Thinking Skills through Science*. London: Taylor & Francis.

Wallace, B., Maker, J. and Zimmerman (2008). *Thinking Activity in a Social Context: Theory and Practice*, Sheffield: TASC.

Williams, E. and Shuard H. (1994) *Primary Mathematics Today,* London: Longman.

Warwick, P. and Dawes, L. (2013) Science, in R. Jones and D. Wyse, D. (eds.) Creativity in the Primary Curriculum (2nd edn.). London: David Fulton.Williams, E. and Shuard, H. (1994) *Primary Mathematics Today* (4th edn.). Harlow: Longman.

Williams, P. (2008) *Independent Review of Mathematics Teaching in Early Years Settings and Schools*. London: DCSF.

Index